Bent Hope

Bent Hope

a street journal

Tim Huff

Foreword by Michael Frost

Benediction by Steve Bell

Bent Hope: A Street Journal

Copyright ©2008 Tim J. Huff
All rights reserved
Printed in Canada
International Standard Book Number: 978-1-894860-36-9

Published by:
Castle Quay Books
1-1295 Wharf Street, Pickering, Ontario, L1W 1A2
Tel: (416) 573-3249   Fax: (416) 981-7922
E-mail: info@castlequaybooks.com
www.castlequaybooks.com

Written by Tim J. Huff
Foreword by Michael Frost
Benediction by Steve Bell
Copy editing by Marla Konrad
Proof reading by Julia Beazley and Marina H. Hofman
Cover Design by Gordon Brew of Thinkhouse Design
Printed at Essence Publishing, Belleville, Ontario

Library and Archives Canada Cataloguing in Publication

Huff, Tim, 1964-

Bent hope : a street journal / Tim J. Huff.

ISBN 978-1-894860-36-9

1. Church work with the homeless--Ontario--Toronto. 2. Homeless persons--Ontario--Toronto. I. Title.

BV4456.H82 2008   261.8'32509713541   C2008-900740-9

CASTLE QUAY BOOKS

Table of Contents

Author's Acknowledgements

Bent Hope

To my wonderful wife Diane, and fantastic children—Sarah Jane and Jake: Words do no justice to the love, appreciation and admiration I have for you. Our home has always been a place of peace, comfort, joy, and healing because of your astounding sacrifice, love and laughter. Thank you for filling me up every single day. I cherish you beyond measure.

Thank you to my dear parents (Arlene and Liv), my brothers (Liv Jr. and Dan) and their steadfast families, and the Johnson family—for their continuous love and support.

As I set out to write this book, I invited a small group of thinkers, readers, writers and artists to serve as a sounding-board/focus-group over a two year period—reflecting on each chapter and providing feedback along the way; friends that I admire in countless ways. My great thanks to: Miller Alloway—for remarkable vision and generosity. Julia Beazley—for sharing your incredible heart, soul and giftedness. Steve Bell—for inspiring me with astounding talent and friendship. Laura Jane Brew—for endless trust, laughter and encouragement. Alan Davey—for speaking great truth with great humility. Michael Frost—for the support of kinship and challenging me to newness. Sharon Gernon—for loving unconditionally. John McAuley—for exemplifying excellence in all things. Greg Paul—for brotherhood. Rick Tobias—for great faithfulness and conviction. John Wilkinson—for modeling leadership and friendship with a true servant's heart.

An additional small group of friends and loved ones were entrusted with the original manuscript before it reached editing. Thank you for your feedback, encouragement and care: Tina and Mike Barlow, Randy Barnetson, Cheryl Bear, Annie Brandner, MacKenzie Brock, Karen Clausen, Lydia Clinton, Jocelyn Durston, Teres Edmonds, Adrienne Grant, Kristy Grisdale, Alan Hirsch, Annette Jones, Steve Kennedy, Sue and Mark Kocaurek, Sarah Lester, Jennine Loewen, Barry Pettit, Heather Ploeg, and Angela Porter.

Acknowledgements

Many thanks to my friends at Ark Outreach, Bridgeway, Crossroads, The Dam, Daily Bread Food Bank, EFC, Frontlines, The Gateway, Harvest House, Hockey For The Homeless, Inner-city Youth Alive, The Ladybug Foundation, Lightworks, Living Rock, Mastermind Educational, Mission Services of London, Matthew House, Muskoka Woods, The Mustard Seed, One Way Inn, Ontario Camp of the Deaf, Ottawa Inner-City Ministries, On Rock, Salvation Army, Sanctuary, Scott Mission, Second Harvest, Siloam Mission, Sketch, StreetLevel: The National Roundtable on Poverty and Homelessness, Streetlight, Toronto City Mission, Urban Promise, World Vision, YFC chapters across Canada, USA and worldwide, Yonge Street Mission, YSM's Evergreen, and YWAM.

It is an honour to serve among people who faithfully give so much of themselves. Thank you to the incredibly devoted Light Patrol team, the entire Youth Unlimited (Toronto YFC) staff and board, as well as the many supporters—individuals, families, churches and businesses—who have stood with me in countless ways, for many years.

They say it takes a village to raise a child. As it turns out, it takes several villages to raise a street outreach worker. One of these vital villages for me has been Weston Park Baptist Church. I am so thankful for my many dear friends (far too many to list)—past and present, from my youth through adulthood—from Weston Park.

In addition to those already mentioned, I am indebted to these faithful friends for helping in one way or another to keep my head above water: David Adcock, Cynthia Barlow, Carol Brown, Karen Chambers, Dale Cheslock, David Collison, Marianne Deeks, Cathy Dienesch, Sandra Groves, Mel Hems, Denise Holland, Mike Leney, Gail and Bill Masson, Lori McAuley, Dawn Curnew-Millar, John Mohan, Carl Nash, Pat Nixon, Dion Oxford, Linda Revie, Paul Robertson, the entire and extended Rumball family, Fay and Don Simmonds, Lori Holtam-Weedon, Haidee and David White, Linda Wisz, and my band buddies in both Outrider and Double Edge.

My heartfelt thanks to Larry Willard at Castle Quay Books Canada—for his steadfast commitment and enthusiasm.

A very special thanks to Julia Beazley—once again, for her tireless dedication and faithfulness to the entire Bent Hope project, in so many capacities, from start to finish. Priceless! (Even providing the author's photo.)

My sincere thanks to: Marla Konrad—for her warm and professional approach to the material through the editing stage, and for her great encouragement to me. Marina Hofman at Castle Quay Books Canada—for her keen

Acknowledgements

work and energy. Gord Brew and the Thinkhouse Design staff—for capturing the essence of the book, and for great commitment to the whole project.

My humble thanks to Miller and Terri Alloway and family, and the Maranatha Foundation for sponsoring priceless time away to complete this book, and for supporting its launch and release.

It is such a privilege to have the thoughtful voices of musicians, authors, speakers, spiritual leaders and visionaries sharing in the Bent Hope chapter-by-chapter prayers of reflection found at www.signpostvillage.com/timhuff : Judy and Pierre Allard, Miller Alloway, Cheryl Bear, Julia Beazley, Steve Bell, Bruxy Cavey, Alan Davey, Michael Frost, Adrienne Grant, Mike Janzen, Marla Konrad, Drew Marshall, Colin McCartney, John McAuley, Jacob Moon, Sister Sue Mosteller, Dion Oxford, Greg Paul, Glen Soderholm, Rick Tobias, Dave Toycen, John Wilkinson, and Larry Willard.

This book is dedicated to my dear friends from the street. The ones I said goodbye to, the ones I didn't get to, the ones long ago, the ones still there, the young, the old, the terrified, the courageous, those who made me laugh, those who made me cry, and all those who did both. Thank you for teaching me, sharing with me, challenging me, stirring me, and making every moment feel urgent and priceless. God bless all those surviving the streets this very moment. I pray that home finds you, even when you can't find home.

Foreword

By Michael Frost

Tim Huff is a hopeful man. Not even twenty years of frozen pavements can dull his relentless, twisted, not-quite-right hopefulness. Not twenty years of runaways, overdoses, hunger, anger, violence or injustice. Not two whole decades of suffering and sadness. Hope keeps floating to the surface despite every attempt to sink it on the streets of Toronto. The evidence of this might very well be the book you are holding, but for those of us who know and love Tim, it only takes one glance at his crooked smile to sense the bent hope that sustains him and inspires others. At least now with this book, Tim's instinct for finding hope in unlikely places is available to those not fortunate enough to have walked Yonge Street with him.

Those who wade chest-deep into the world of the poor can end up being submerged in cynicism and suspicion, so intractable seem the social conditions that give rise to such inequity. And yet the cumulative effect of Tim's stories is the realization that when we truly know that Jesus lives among and loves the poor, the more likely outcome of plunging into their world is the recovery of the gift of hope.

This gift of hope is not merely the naïve sense that everything will work out all right in the end. It's deeper and richer. People who hope in the face of poverty and injustice know Jesus' preference for the poor and have managed to muster enough confidence in his coming kingdom, a world of order, peace, security, justice and abundance. These hope-filled ones don't deny the present disorder, with its confusion and distortion. How could anyone who walks the late-night streets of any big city deny the chaos? But they hope, watch, wait, pray and expect, knowing that Jesus' scheme for the future is reliable and trustworthy. And they act upon it before it is fully in hand.

How do you act on the future before it is in hand? The hope-filled ones ask themselves: if Jesus' future kingdom is secure, what needs to happen now? And the answer is: Jesus' future kingdom is enacted now as *neighbourliness*. With hope as our guide, we are called to fashion traces of the coming kingdom right now, and one of the primary ways to do that is by the practice of good neighbourliness.

When asked which was the most important commandment, Jesus said, "Love God and love your neighbour." Have you ever noticed that, though he was asked for *the* most important commandment, he gives them two? It's as if he's saying, "You cannot have one without the other. With God you always get the neighbour as well." Now we live in a society that wants to separate God from neighbourliness, but you can't claim to love God without the neighbour. In Jesus' vision of the world, they are a package deal. So, in a kingdom of neighbourliness the homeless, the widow, the orphan, the illegal immigrant, the poor and the disabled all count. They become agents of hope, opportunities for us to express our confidence in the coming kingdom, rather than threats or inconveniences.

Too bad that for many the people whose stories are collected in this volume are just that—threats and inconveniences. Too bad that there aren't more people with Tim Huff's bent hope who can see the opportunities for neighbourliness they represent. They are all citizens of God's shalom. They count in Christ's here-and-still-coming kingdom every bit as much as we do.

Tim quotes Emily Dickinson's allusion to hope as "...the thing with feathers / That perches in the soul, / And sings the tune—without the words, / And never stops at all."

And never stops at all! That's quite a thing. Surely, the birdsong of hope sings in the soul of someone like Tim Huff. His simple but resolute choice to be a good neighbour to the poor of Toronto summons up the kingdom, bringing its future consummation forward into the here and now, creating foretastes of the fullness yet to come and flipping the bird to those who want to shape our present reality according to their selfishness, greed and fear.

Let me warn you that as you read this street journal it will dawn on you at some point that this is not a book on how to serve the poor, though it's certainly written by a servant to the poor. It will also dawn on you that this is not simply a collection of snapshots of life on the mean streets of a major urban centre, though you will meet bag ladies, beggars and runaways. Let me warn you that if you read it correctly and this book works its way into your soul, you'll realize at some point that this is a book about the beauty, the wonder and the holiness of all humanity, even the bent-out-of-shape ones. By revealing the refracted rays of hope that can be found among the "least of these," Tim Huff shines light on us all. If hope can be found within the broken, the betrayed, the abandoned and the frightened, then where *can't* it be found?!

My hope is that in reading this slim volume, you will not just see the poor afresh or your city afresh, but that you'd see yourself afresh, and that you'd follow the birdsong of hope wherever it might lead you, deeper into Jesus' kingdom of neighbourliness.

Michael Frost

Michael Frost is the author of several best-selling books and one of Australia's most widely recognized contemporary theological speakers in his own country and around the world, having spoken at some of the largest conventions and events throughout Australia, North America, Europe, Asia and Africa. Michael is the Founding Director of the Centre for Evangelism & Global Mission at Morling Theological College in Sydney and is strongly committed to leadership development, serving on the board of the Australian Arrow Leadership Development Program and as co-director in the establishment of Forge—a missional training network for young leaders based in Melbourne. Michael has also planted a missional church on Sydney's northern beaches called Small Boat, Big Sea.

The stories in this book are stories of hope. Bent hope. But hope all the same. A couple occur outside of Toronto's city limits and even across the Atlantic, but for the most part they are stories from a good city that unwittingly draws Canada's largest pilgrimage of runaways, hideaways, castaways and throwaways, from small towns and large cities across the nation and even the United States. They are not stories of linear hope that point to magnificent and instant resolve. Not stories that look heavenward in anticipation of the sky cracking open and spilling angels to earth while harps play. But they are true stories of a miraculous finger-of-God hope that exists against all odds, only because the dear souls of these stories are survivors, and heroes and God's own children—forced to seek out hope moment by moment. No more the stories of beggars, hookers and junkies than mine or yours should be.

The awkward truth can be packed into a single crass statement:

Either we are all beggars, hookers and junkies, or none of us are. There is no in-between.

At times—and for some, all the time—we all live with the cruel designations others have carelessly tattooed on us. Subjugated by what others think we are, and oppressed by what we feel stuck doing or being, while our hearts and minds long for release.

Every day I play the role of a beggar. I look to the charity of others, seemingly wanting something for nothing to feed my ego and the overwhelming need to belong. Every day I play the role of a hooker. I try to sell the words, ideas and actions I think might make me desirable to others, often against my own better judgment, in order to get the emotional validation I need to survive. And every day I play the role of a junkie. I feed my addictions, supplying relentless cravings with products, entertainment, daydreams and relationships that are bad for me. Thus, when rendered solely in vulgar human slang, I believe we are all beggars, hookers and junkies. And if raw humanity existed as the only gauge, I would know for certain that I am all of these.

But long before our biases and jaded opinions develop, long before we categorize people with labels and by issues, we all start in the same place, with the wide-eyed innocence and acceptance of childhood.

While this book is filled with gritty street stories, my desire is that no one would feel distant to its heartbeat. And so, it is in the tender memories of childhood that I begin. My own childhood comprehension of hope was similar to that of most children. *Wishful* and *lucky*–that's hope. I was wrong.

It was while walking along the mom-forbidden railway tracks to elementary school that I best recall hope revealing itself to me in an entirely new way. I came across an orange tabby cat lying in a ball, thrown several body-lengths from the rails. Even as I approached from a distance, it was clear what had happened. One of the racing trains that crossed the rails had ended the life of someone's dear pet. As a child, I approached it with that strange mix of emotions that stir inside most people as they view a calamity: the ridiculous and ugly combination of sorrow and curiosity.

Mesmerized, I stood over the cat's motionless body, bending closer, and then closer again, for a more graphic take on the situation. After several minutes of sorrowful investigation, I stepped away, back towards the stiff weeds in the ditch. As I stood silent in my disbelief, I heard a soft wee voice crying out in two-tone notes. I tiptoed cautiously through the wild grass towards the tiny voice. As I headed further into the low brush I began to hear a second tiny voice singing in sad harmony. With little-boy steps in rubber-toed sneakers, I circled around until I found the source. Two tiny kittens. Small white faces peering up from green and gold thickets, calling out for the assurance of their protector and provider. But she would not answer. Beauty in tragedy. Tragedy in beauty.

I lifted them gently into my arms one by one, and as I did they called out louder and louder. They quivered and squirmed as I rocked them slowly– talking to myself all the while. Surely I could take them home. But what story could I make up? What story should I make up? I could not tell my mom and dad that I had been walking where I had been told so many times not to go. Even at a young age, I had a history of dangerous mischief along the railway tracks. And still, I thought–would they be so moved by the situation, and so caught up in these adorable creatures that they wouldn't care and would overlook my disobedience? Better yet, would a white lie be justified in this case, all the same? I held the kittens for a long time and tried to hatch a plan. But soon enough I recognized that I was very late for school and was losing confidence in my ability to make myself the inventive storyteller who might get to keep the kittens.

So I set them back down in the thick blades of crabgrass and just stared at them. I stared with that look people get when their hearts tell them to do what's right, and their heads tell them the cost is too high—that sustained look that eventually reveals that the head is self-serving enough to win the battle.

Then I began to ask their forgiveness. I promised them that something good would surely happen; an eight-year-old's weak poke of hope. I even prayed for them, with a very earnest little boy's "Hey God, let's make a deal" prayer. And then I tried to walk away, my young soul weighted down with what can only be described as *the hurt of hope.*

Three or four steps at best. Halted by the chiming sounds of tiny kittens floating up from the wild grass and creeping weeds. I remember the hurt of hoping something wonderful would happen. Something magic. Something surprising and instant.

Then, from far off, just beneath the kitten calls, I heard a voice. Repetitive, monotone, and from a distance, sounding at first like a hum more than words.

"Oh no. Oh no. Oh no. Oh no."

All of a sudden, cutting through the wide slats in a backyard fence, was a woman in a pale yellow apron. She stumbled down the steep mound, with her hands over her mouth, staring at her dead cat.

"But the kittens are right here," I blurted out, gesturing enthusiastically towards the tall grass.

"Oh no. Oh no. Oh no. Oh no." All these years later, I can still hear her responding with a trembling and somehow heroic, "Oh no."

Her face was round and warm, even in her grand upset. Her small eyes darted from the motionless cat to the chirping twin kittens, to the mischievous little boy trying to stand invisible in front of her. A second survey of the images before her, and an all-knowing grown-up nod followed. She picked up the kittens lovingly and put one in each of the big pockets of her worn apron, reprimanded me sternly for being on the dangerous railway, turned sharply and shuffled her way up the hill, between the broken fence planks, and into her yard. All the while, fading out of sight with, "Oh no. Oh no. Oh no. Oh no," until her voice was nothing more than a hum again.

It's just a childhood story. Not unlike adventures that many boys and girls might recall. Still, the little-boy panic of not knowing what to do, or how to make things better, finds me time and time again all through my adulthood. I have left countless young people lost and alone in the frightening long grass, only steps away from imminent danger. I have avoided hundreds of mentally ill adults because I was late for a happier and simpler destination. I have justified staying uninvolved countless times, in countless situations, because the cost seemed too high. I have prayed, wished and begged God for miracles thousands of times on the streets, under bridges, in dark alleyways and in my own back-yard. And I have lost by now what must literally count as years of sleep to the hurt of hope.

And still, in spite of myself, *the hurt of hope*, along with *the anticipation of hope*, and *hope realized* are all at the center of the lives I have been so honoured to be a part of on the streets.

The upset "oh no's" of that busy homemaker scurrying about were a won-derful part of the music that day, for a little boy late for grade three. And even more so for the two tabby kittens that ended up nestled in her soft apron pockets. Yes, it was a glorious bit of music in the mind of child who has carried that tune in his head his entire life.

Surely *hope* is the music of the soul. Sometimes passionate and wild. Sometimes simple and melodic. Frequently out of tune and unrehearsed. And quite often found in the glorious "oh no's" of an anxious loved one yearning to fix things and willing to do anything.

How profound and supernatural is it when it is more than even these. Somewhere in the miracle of survival, hope at its astounding best is life-giving. I have been blessed, shocked and severely scarred throughout my years on the street to see, hear and share in hope that is relentlessly life-giving and life-changing. The stories in the chapters that follow, both beautiful and tragic, bear witness to that.

Just as music wraps itself around a moment, a day or even a season, hope lifts, pauses, jolts and abounds in operatic proportions. The breathtaking *anticipation of hope* can be hypnotic as one senses the buds of health, progress or opportunity about to open. And *hope realized* is that grand inhale that fills the lungs in the final millisecond when someone escapes suffocation.

But it is the *hurt of hope* that is often the thorn too deep in the skin to dig out. In the midst of my own insecurities and hurts—the ones that have sucker-punched and taunted me throughout my life—I am floored by what I can only imagine are the overwhelming memories, hurts and abuses that grip my friends on the street. If I can recall 15 minutes of gentle sadness on the way to elementary school, how do the deviant sexual atrocities of an abusive father cripple a girl as she tries to grow up? How does the drunken fist of an angry parent stay with a boy as he stumbles into manhood? How do any of us carry on when our protectors have perished, like a cat struck by a train? When hope is not realized because of the horrors of abuse, isolation, and the loss of those who were supposed to love you, why would you continue to hope? When you have done all you can to find your way, and have only found abandonment, pain, loneliness and fear, why would you dare to hope? When the music of hope is drowned out by the noise of a death march, why not shut the music off forever?

Words do it no justice, perhaps because the hum of hope is gentle and healing. The purr of a harmonious calling. The early resonance of a sound-track for binding up the brokenhearted in which the hurt of hope can be soothed.

But just as the splendor of music can be diminished by simple disregard and disrespect, hope can be grotesquely distorted and warped. Nothing squelches hope like an onlooker's arrogance and pride. Nothing mugs hope like lukewarm pity. And nothing spoils hope like ignorance. All too often, those of us who have been spared the unthinkable tragedies of chronic abuse, isolation, addiction and rejection expect simple answers from those who have experienced these incredible hurts. "What happened? What will fix it? And what will it cost?" We want them to sum up the problems and give us the answers. Waiting in the wings for the answers we like, with timelines we deem reasonable. Answers we can claim and endorse when they fit our values and agendas, when in fact the true hum of hope includes the silent and spectacular victories of simply making it through another day.

Hidden in the cloak of daily survival and existence is where hope plays its most significant role. In the fatigue and discouragement of all-day-ness and every-day-ness—this is when hope is the anchor that keeps life from being swept away. We cannot wait until lives become epic, movie-ending creations. It's so easy to exploit someone else's life story by manipulating it into a nice neat package. A package we want boxed, bowed and presented without ever having been near their pain or the battle that, more often than not, secretly rages on. Counting on people to simply rise up and start over like cats with nine lives.

But cats only have one life, and hope doesn't work that way. Real hope transcends all measurement only when we share in it. Not when we simply attempt to watch it magically occur in someone's life, or wish for it from a distance, but when we participate in it. Not when we simply hear the humming, but when we hum along.

Hope, says Webster, is "The virtue by which a Christian looks with confidence for God's grace in this world and glory in the next."

My heart hears it like this:

Confidence: the reshaping of hope from a passive, wishful notion to its rightful place; the pitch-perfect bass line of hope's song.

Grace: the sweet extension of hope borne out of the brokenness that each of us owns; the captivating melody of hope's song.

Glory: the certainty that God has an astounding plan and celebration that reaches far beyond what we can even begin to fathom; the thrilling crescendo of hope's song.

Confidence, grace and glory that include all boys and girls, men and women; built on the firm foundation of being in relationship with the life-giver. The very place where I believe God extended himself so that I could know for sure that hope is real was in a homeless baby born in a stable, who grew to promise the hope of abundant life, before he sacrificed his own. Abundant life is without a doubt the most undervalued and unappreciated promise ever made.

Even as I share these thoughts at the outset of this book, I fear two things. That those who call themselves Christians or "Jesus Followers" will assume this book is just for them. And that those who don't will assume it is for someone else.

But this is not so. What follows is extended to all for consideration, deliberation and reflection: those who believe there is no God, those who hate God, those who struggle with God, those who believe in another one, and those who believe in him as Abba Father alike, convicted by an incredible remark made by Mahatma Gandhi: "If Christians would really live according to the teachings of Christ, found in the Bible, all of India would be Christian today."

In spite of my own astounding inadequacies as a Christian and a human being, my faith is based solely on Jesus Christ. Not on Christians. Not a single one. And while I believe he was and is the Son of God, many of those I know who think he was just a great man can't help but agree that he is a role model beyond compare.

Ultimately I believe in a God who is as relevant in the gutter as he is in the church. As miraculous in the ditch as he is in the chapel. And as beautiful in a rat-infested alleyway as he is in a glass cathedral. Anything else is hopeless. And nothing else makes sense.

I have no theological degrees or formal religious studies. I attended two community colleges in unrelated studies, and graduated from one. My beliefs and theories are born out of an education I had not anticipated as a young man: sneaking through crack-houses, weeping at hospital bedsides, strolling through alleyways after midnight, gigging at biker rallies, empathizing through prison bars, waiting at bus terminals, explaining myself in police stations, laughing beneath bridges, tripping through abandoned buildings, peeking into squats and shanties, leaning into gullies and ditches, serving at a camp for deaf children, living as a family man, and more than four decades of taking in Sunday mornings from the first five pews of a very decent, century-old church at the crossroads of a volatile community.

While I have occasionally altered names and locations to guard identities, these pages reveal snapshots of real times and places, bodies and faces, sonnets and odes that could easily be lost in the shadows of a population too hurried to notice. Fragmented glimpses of fragmented lives, where hope is anything but shiny and bright. Unpolished. Crushed. Twisted. Bent hope.

But somewhere in the wrinkles of every brief account, hope continues to hum. It continues to breathe. Often shallow breaths at best; even the faintest final breath, whispering one more note in the music of the soul.

Bent hope—inviting us all to be part of the music.

December 2005

"Hope is a passion for what is possible."

I should think the last image in Søren Kierkegaard's mind when he wrote this statement more than a century and a half ago was a panicked boy swimming in the sewer water of the most multicultural city in the world. And still the philosopher's words were undeniably, even if unexpectedly, a tailor-made fit for the boy, the time and the place.

Thomas's body was covered in sludge. Long dark trails of brown, clumps of black, and a glaze of translucent yellow. His shirt and socks were rolled in sopping balls lying next to his curled sneakers. Everything soaked. Everything shriveled and dirty. Ripe with the stench of waste and toxins. High on a flat rock, facing the unfamiliar pool below—a boy, just a boy, who had lost everything.

The summer of 2005 went on record as the hottest in decades. Showers and breezes were elusive at best. Far away from the mid-winter gasps of street sympathizers—"Oh, the cold, this cold, surely this deadly cold is the worst of all worsts!" That is the pebble in the shoe of every mind that stops to consider homelessness across Canada and in the northern United States. Around the

Chapter 1

beginning of February, people who ask me nothing about my homeless friends all year long will inevitably ask, "How do they survive? How do they bear it?" And no doubt, it takes the fortitude and will of a prize-winning bull to push through it.

But lost on most people, more often than not, is what it takes to survive the heat. Not just heat...but inner-city heat. Heat that not only comes from above, but from below. The sandwich heat that traps a body between the sky's ball of fire at full volume from above and the hellish pavement and concrete from below. Endless baking pavement. Endless simmering concrete. Endless heat that refuses to let up. Captured in the day and stored in the solar tar by night.

This was the oppressive heat that drove Thomas to the Don River. One of the few stretches anywhere near the city core that reveals more green than grey. A seam through the city where a dull wind can find its way north and south, to and from Lake Ontario. And just enough murky water that when one squints his or her eyes a bit of elsewhere-ness can be imagined.

Not clean water. Certainly not healthy water. But water all the same. The Don has been abused like most urban rivers. Early in the twentieth century, industries such as paint factories and paper mills bled their waste into the river. As did more than 30 sewage treatment plants. Though much effort over the past few decades has gone into bettering the river and surrounding forest lines, even now, storm water is the primary source of the river's pollution. It makes up nearly three-quarters of the river's flow—and carries the waste migrating from freeways and driveways, backyards and truckyards. Untreated and directly into the waterway.

Still, for Thomas, there was plenty of leafy shade there. Mature trees and a sense of oxygen, non-existent in the core of the city. A bit of resistance to the conquering sun. Thomas was there, in the shade of a shrub, counting change from a coffee cup, when the sky was finally squeezed. Not a gentle squeeze. Certainly not an anticipated one. It was a shocking bear hug from behind. What one television weather anchor called a "spontaneous late-summer torrential macro-burst." What simply felt like the inevitable result of a demolished dam hidden beyond the clouds. It didn't rain in drops. Or even buckets. It came down in thick sheets of blinding, pounding rain. Apocalyptic rain, both unpredicted and unforgiving.

That same Don River runs in tandem to the Don Valley Parkway; the city's only freeway running north and south. The rolling motorway dips deep near the river in several spots resulting in enormous flash-flood zones during severe downpours.

A Kid and a Coffee Cup

On this day, the rain simply had nowhere to go once it landed. In addition, the excess streamed into the natural basins from the ill-equipped sewer system. One of the great dim pools rose beneath the unofficial sky-high border to "downtown proper"; The Bloor Viaduct, known well for its history of suicide jumpers. Right where Thomas was.

The late night television news would ultimately show police on jet-skis and wave-runners, rescuing stranded drivers who had abandoned their submerged automobiles and shimmied onto concrete bulkheads. Homes some 20 kilometres north had basements under four, six, and eight feet of water. All of it charged in, had its tantrum, and hissy-fitted away without warning. Thomas, nestled in his remote pocket of wilderness, was caught off guard as much as any homeowner with satellite TV and access to weather forecasts by the minute. Heat, heat, heat...then with the city worn into submission, the clouds dropped a black curtain, flexed their muscles and said "gotcha!"

Somewhere between the mystery of it all and thanksgiving for cool relief, Thomas was besieged by the volume and incredible speed of the rising water. As crisp grass and dry soil softened and bloated the sloping hills, things began to float. Then bob, then swirl, then escape. Literally within minutes the river swelled and surged over the banks. And Thomas—young Thomas—panicked his way through the gloomy undertow on a desperate retrieval mission.

When I arrived long after the flood, Thomas was rolled in a ball on a dry rock slate, weeping. He had been a severe victim of the storm. As is usually the case for the forgotten few—the forgotten too-many—absent of both "home" and shelter. But his absence of everything caught me off guard. Every single thing. No backpack? No sleeping bag? So few items to maintain and save? Items so at-hand. As rapid as it was, it was not as though he was struck by a tidal wave. How? How did the boy who had so little now have nothing?

I was eager to ask. But I was not sure how to do it without sounding con-descending. So, I just sat beside him. He wept and I just sat. For a long, long time. No words. Just the unnerving sense that there was far more to his tears than I knew.

"We can get stuff, new stuff, better stuff...whatever you need," I babbled.

"Maybe this is a good time to try another route. Find you a place," I continued, committed to the exhausting philosophy that long-term success in guiding young, severely broken lives into healthy adulthoods best, and almost always, starts with trust. Then moves to action. No matter how long that takes. The "absolute" I have indoctrinated myself with, and committed to, for better or worse.

But he heard none of it. He was not purposely ignoring me. Just crying so intensely that he literally could not hear me. So I waited while he sobbed, oblivious of my presence or the passing of time. My fierce curiosity and eagerness to intervene begrudgingly gave way to the better judgment of allowing him his time. His grief. His desperation.

Sirens echoed in and out of earshot forever as we sat side by side in silence. The awkward sounds of others getting help, others mattering, others inconvenienced.

Finally a long shaky sigh.

"My sister. My, my...."

Then more tears. More time. And several more sirens clearing their throats in the distance—heard and not seen. Everyone else getting fixed up.

"My sister was 14 when she left. Now how will I remember her? How will I find her?"

Thomas carried her picture in his fanny pack. She was two years younger than Thomas, but escaped their abusive home a year earlier than he did.

While the waters gobbled up all of his belongings, Thomas sacrificed it all for a search-and-rescue mission through the mire. Desperate for the eight-inch sack that housed the image of his sister.

His grief was shocking. His response was on par with that of a death, rather than the loss of a photograph. His heart broke open and his grieving words dribbled out.

"I was in the park. Waiting, just waiting! I should have been there! I should have been there!"

The critical history, in short, was this: while Thomas was waiting out his father's rabid drunkenness—waiting for it to submit to a state of unconsciousness—his sister hit the unavoidable wall that comes with the fatigue of chronic abuse. She left a picture on Thomas's bed as she snuck away. On the back of it she wrote:

I'll die here. One day come and find me. I love you.

"How will I remember her? How will I find her? How...how...how...," his weak body collapsed and he sprawled back, arched along the shiny rock face.

Who are the homeless?

Why are they like that?

Why don't they just go home? Or go somewhere else?

They're pathetic.

They're ruining the city.

Delinquents. Lazy. Troublemakers.

Hideous.

A Kid and a Coffee Cup

After all of these years I have heard everything. Every question, every assertion, every concern, every query, every self-righteous and self-absorbed commentary. On the streets, in office buildings, at luncheons in church basements. But stuck in the moment, sitting beside soaking, stinking, exhausted, torn-apart, magnificent Thomas, all I wanted to do was hunt down every person I had ever heard spout out their uncompassionate ignorance and scream into their faces. Scream them away.

It happens often. And usually lasts until I bump into my own hypocrisy. When God allows it to drop-kick me off my feet. When I remember the guy on the crammed subway who bugged me by flopping around fast asleep in his seat. The girl at the convenience store I thought was kind of dopey because she was taking too long counting my change. The well-dressed kids bumming smokes outside the corner store that I shake my head at. Me. Me indeed. Me not embracing the very song I sing whenever I am asked about those I know on the street:

EVERY PERSON HAS THEIR OWN STORY.

To see muddy, messed-up Thomas sitting curbside, drinking from dented pop cans left half-full in trash bins, the quickest assumption made is that "he's a problem." He looks like a problem. Smells like a problem. For sure, he and all those like him are a problematic black eye on tourism. A problem for store owners, city council, family restaurants and fancy hotels. Some think he's the mayor's problem. Some think he's the police's problem. Provincial problem. Federal problem. Maybe he was the liquor store's problem? The next-door neighbour who looked the other way's problem? The teacher who didn't report the obvious bruises' problem? The downsizing employer who laid off his dad's problem? The hospital that couldn't cure his sick mom's problem? The church at the end of his street's problem? Messy, messed-up Thomas was the poster boy for pass-the-buck finger-pointing from every direction. He just thought he was a kid tired of getting beat up in his kitchen. Until he left. Then people made sure he knew what he really was. Not sure of whose. But sure of what.

A big problem!

But what about his story! His incredible story! It is his. The story of a heart that should be a brick but never hardened. The story of salvaging love and keeping promises. The story of broken bottles, broken limbs and a broken heart. His, his and his. All parts of his story. One of only two things that any of us possess that is truly priceless. One is our time. The other is our story. Each one one-of-a-kind. No less than the sleepy man on public transit, the sweet girl doing her best with simple mathematics or the wealthy teenagers looking for

Chapter 1

something more. The ones I jump to conclusions over. The good, the bad and the ugly. They all have a story. Their own story.

Only days later, Hurricane Katrina devastated the delta expanses while terrorizing the Northwest Gulf of Mexico and hypnotizing an entire continent. The worst natural disaster on record in the United States of America. Thomas and I watched it on CNN through an electronics store window, alarmed at the pictures and headlines. Unable to hear the reports, aghast at the images, we followed the headers at the top of the screen. Thomas was in tears. Not the same desperate tears of stabbing grief shed days earlier. Thoughtful, quiet tears.

Two days after Katrina's assault on the deep south, Thomas spotted me coming up from the subway tunnel.

He ran towards me excitedly, "Tim, Tim, I need your help!"

At last! These are the words cherished most by me. Symbols of trust and signs of hope.

I nodded and shrugged my shoulders, "Sure!"

My mind began to race. Which shelter? Which contact? Maybe Evergreen's Health Centre first? It's the best. Maybe Covenant House next? A roof, a bed. I was readying my arsenal of help suggestions for baby step number one.

But before I could say a thing, he lifted his hand towards me. In it was a weathered old coffee cup. A Tim Horton's coffee cup; the contemporary symbol of Canadiana from farm gates to skyscrapers, coast to coast. It was filled with change.

Dimes, pennies, nickels, quarters and the Canadian coins that make panhandling a tad more promising—one dollar "loonies" and two dollar "toonies." They rattled and slid side-to-side just below the brim as he shook his hand proudly. I looked at him curiously as he waved the cup in front of me, gesturing for me to take it. He grinned wide, enjoying the suspense he held over me. His smile was toothy and bright, and his eyes were more alive than I had ever seen them.

Finally, with his other hand, he reached into his back pocket and pulled out a crumpled piece of ribbed cardboard, about the size of a shoebox top. He held it beside the coffee cup, only inches from my face.

With poetic beauty, in big scratchy letters created by the feverish dedication of scribbling a ballpoint back and forth over and over again, it read:

"For Katrina's homeless, because it hurts to lose everything."

The help he wanted? For me to take him to the bank. Just to make sure they would let him in so he could give it to the teller. That was it.

So I did. I took him. There was a long line. We waited for our turn, taking small steps every few minutes through the velvet-rope maze. The people in front of us and behind us kept a ridiculous distance away. Thomas pretended not to notice.

Finally we were next. He placed the cup on the counter in front of the teller. She looked down at it and wrinkled up her nose. Then looked up at him. Bewildered, she cocked her head and glanced at me. I tugged the sign out of Thomas's back pocket and laid it on the counter beside the cup. The teller's eyes welled up, and she smiled gently. She lifted the cup carefully with both hands and nodded.

"Can you add it to what's been collected," Thomas asked like a wide-eyed little boy.

"I will," the teller promised softly. "Yes, I will."

We turned. We walked away.

This is Thomas's story. This is who Thomas is. Who he really is. This is who I need to be, who we all need to be. This is the personification of Kierkegaard's brilliant and simple description of hope; a boy—a boy with nothing to his name—passionate about the possibility of making a difference. Regardless of the circumstances and obstacles.

The hot days grew cool, and the cool days grew cold. Thomas braved the change of seasons with a sense of newness. Something changed inside of him when his heart broke for others, regardless of his own plight. In his own brokenness he found his identity. Thomas found the best of who he was, and refused to ignore it. The best of who God had made him. An authentic, beautiful identity that people spend a lifetime looking for. One only ever found by sacrificing. No one needed the money in that coffee cup more than Thomas.

He took independent steps towards wellness. He began saying quirky and inspirational things like "God has a plan, y'know?" At first just to tease and appease me, for sure. But not much time passed before he said it with conviction. He secured a room all on his own. Then a better room and some financial assistance. Then some work. All without my help. God had led me to do but one important thing early in the process. That one thing was simply to be in the presence of Thomas's astounding compassion and generosity. To receive the gift of knowing and being with Thomas. Ultimately, just to stand beside a poor boy in front of a total stranger while he gladly surrendered his tiny portion of wealth.

Thomas moved himself west just before Christmas. All with his own earned resources. He wanted to follow some hunches on his sister's whereabouts.

But two weeks before he left I saw him sitting outside of Toronto's world-class Hospital For Sick Children. I was surprised to see him there. It wasn't his common turf, and he had not needed to wait on loose change for some time.

The snow was falling lightly, the moment fixed for Norman Rockwell. I stopped about two meters in front of Thomas when my eyes caught sight of the little sign resting beside the coffee cup in front of his crossed legs:

"Donations for Sick Kids. No one should ever lose a sister."

It wasn't about the money. He had his own. It was about giving other people the opportunity to participate in hope as he understood it. It was about Thomas's own turnabout, what triggered it, and his wanting to make it contagious.

Some saw a beggar sitting outside the hospital that day. Some were sure they saw a scam. Many paid no mind as they trudged past a typical downtown object, a cityscape prop on par with a fire hydrant, park bench or trash can. Very few saw one made in the image of God. And none suspected a passion for what is possible.

Most people walking by, if they took notice at all, just saw a kid and a coffee cup.

But there was so much more.

There always is. Always.

October 2003

Raised scars on young wrists have haunted me for years. Lamentably, I know too much. The opportunity to literally and figuratively "read between the lines" has not been lost on me.

A series of tiny slender tracks, criss-crossed along the fleshy part of the forearm, front or back—a desperate call for someone to take notice, or just the desire to feel something. Anything.

Shallow lines that widen from the outside of an upturned wrist to the inside—an in-progress decisiveness to take it seriously.

The reverse, wide to shallow, means fear in the final moments.

When I met her, there was no mistaking these tragic scars and trails. Aggressive long thick lines running diagonally from the base of the thumb, six inches towards the elbow. Instantly, two things were certain.

One: right-hand scars reveal a left-handed cutter. Likely a lefty all 'round.

Two: I am in the presence of a miracle. These are the scars of someone who meant business. And still, somehow, she has life.

Fifteen years old. Timidly petitioning for spare change from strangers, with nothing more than her presence. Little more than a child, sleeping among the fattened gutter rats that creep in and out of the sewers of Chinatown. And dressed in the third-hand beaten wares of women on the street three and four times her age.

There are endless questions that haunt all street and inner-city relief workers: Who is she? Whose is she? And how much more hurt does she have to endure in these years that are meant to be the green years of anticipation and innocence?

As I drew near, I could see four university students in matching varsity jackets gathering around her. They were drunk. Very, very drunk. While I sped into a full run I could see them nudging her with their knees, taunting her, and challenging her to respond. Sitting low on the chipped concrete, with her shoulders folded inward, she did nothing and said nothing. But they persisted, eager in their inebriation for mindless entertainment. A cruel synergy set in motion by the heartless belligerence of total intoxication. My pace quickened. My heart was pounding like a hammer. Her defiance to respond reshaped their foolish laughter into tribal anger. Racing through the staggered traffic, I was barely halfway to my destination when I could see mimicking gestures of the unimaginable. Within seconds they were no longer gestures, but performed acts. Snarling and grunting, one of them undid the front of his pants and began urinating on her, while the others cheered him on. She leaned forward over her knees. Her yellow hair tumbled around her shoulders as she simply hung her head to protect her eyes from the stinging pain of physical and emotional abuse.

Consumed by an anger I cannot remember before or since, I arrived throwing punches like I had never imagined. Awkward, fitful punches. A graceless flailing reminiscent of the panicked playground defenses that children use against bullies in elementary school. Hits and misses, anywhere and everywhere. All that the dripping child sitting motionless among us would know for sure, if nothing else, that she was valid of complete outrage.

The entire scenario was disgusting. Drunk and sober humanity graphically revealing every ugly thing but peace. Blood. Drool. Urine. An outreach worker with no recollection of how to de-escalate a volatile situation, and four young men getting off on humiliation. All of it spiraling around a little girl who was living out just one more horrific episode.

The mindless confusion lifted like a slow fog as they finally stumbled away, cursing and laughing. Overwhelmed and outraged, huffing and puffing, I dropped to my knees beside her. She ran the left cuff of her jacket over her mouth, spat out the taste of a stranger's bladder and smiled at me.

Social justice? Contemporary evangelism? Practical ministry? Blah, blah, blah. Words. All just words. Words tossed around like silly treats spilling from a piñata. Candy-coated words that sound tasty in lecture halls and church sanctuaries, and juicy in deep-thinking books. But in the here and now of it all, they just felt like stupid meaningless words, lost in the unforgiving darkness of a child living an undignified life worse than death.

Payback! Revenge! Even *divine wrath!* In the moment these were the words that really made sense. Anything that would lower a boom, and preferably cause some pain.

But if forced to concede to upright and even-keeled words, the best I could do was *righteous anger.* While my behaviour during this hideous incident was ten parts instinct and zero parts prayer, one of the inevitables of the street is living out, and wrestling with, righteous anger. The notion of it alone has kept me sane on many occasions. And while my fit of rage may have been a poor excuse for manifesting righteous anger, and could have gotten me in trouble, I have often justified my actions (for better or worse) by believing that it is godly to be angry when God is angry.

Her slight hands dragged the wet hair from her face. I looked into her eyes with sickening regret, lost for anything meaningful to do or say. And she looked back at me, as though she felt bad for me—that she couldn't make me feel any better. It was a mind-boggling response. She was magnificent in her fortitude.

She continued to dry off her face with the cuff of her torn sleeve, and with a forced smile offered, "It's no big deal."

Revolting! Degrading! Unthinkable! Mortifying! No words, no absurd combination of words could do any justice to what had just occurred. It was a million ridiculous things, and everything except "no big deal!" But so broken, so early in life, these were the first words from the mouth of one of God's own precious children, curled up on a wet curb on an ugly October night. His little miracle, still surviving and surviving and surviving.

Her name was Amy. Soft-spoken and sweet, trying desperately to hide in the camouflage of those who might simply be ignored if they make no fuss. Overlooked by scholars and homemakers, criminals and preachers—hundreds of passersby each day who look down their noses at her with contempt and arrogance.

Very few words later, she looked up at me again with another half smile.

"I'm kind of hungry," she sighed, ever so matter-of-factly.

Amy fumbled through her canvas backpack and pulled out an old brown apple. Bruised and wrinkled. She took a small bite, looked up, and smiled still one more time.

Fifteen. Death scars. Tired eyes. Educated urine in her hair. And the courage to smile; valour that no one can steal. Once again, the miracle of endurance met with the cold effects of numbness. Incongruous and glorious all at once.

Dear Amy. A treasure lost and forgotten. Just one of a legion of sheepish survivors who need to learn to feel again. To believe in more than pain and hurt and humiliation. To have history erased. To truly be 15 years old. And to be honoured over and over again, in this life and in the next, as a child of God.

But on this night, she was having a hard time finding someone who would simply put fifty cents in her empty coffee cup and smile back at her. Makes it more than difficult to believe in the rest. Makes it impossible.

The smell of liquored urine filled the air. I closed my eyes and allowed my mind to throw punches at God, the same way my arms threw them at the drunks. Angrily, awkwardly. But the one-sided fight was interrupted by a sweet voice, ringing with unflappable charity and charm.

"You wanna bite?" She lifted her little brown apple towards me.

Left hand, of course.

May 1995

There is something even more valiant than victory. Something much more gallant found in the person who goes down swinging. Something extraordinary about the resolve to simply keep on keepin' on.

When an ebullient 18-year-old, with a corncob pipe clenched between his teeth, winked at me and, racing after a moving boxcar, called out *"at least I'll go down swinging,"* it was hard not to believe that he would get a lucky shot in before he hit the mat, and somehow at least get a split decision in the prize fight of life. With an adolescent Mickey Rooney charm and an old-school James Cagney tenacity, Smoothy personified the sonnets and fables of hoboism and magically made them his own. A boy who could have lit up the silver screen as a rising star as easily as crawled out from sleeping in a haystack, ready to wander into whatever came next. More character and charisma than any teenager I had ever known.

The term "hobo" became prevalent in the late 1860s, as the U.S. Civil War came to an end, referring to soldiers who were "homeward bound." Most often, by riding the nearly fifty thousand miles of train rail that had been built throughout the United States. By the time World War One ended and the Great Depression had begun, tens of thousands of homeless men, women and children were riding the extensive and rapidly growing web of rails that crisscrossed Canada and the U.S.

As the dramatic history of North America's railways unfolded, hobo culture cultivated its own special folklore. The early twentieth century perceptions (built on both truth and legend) of scary strangers outrunning criminal pasts had widened to include a subculture of harmless wandering homeless people, predominantly men, who would fix a barn door, cobble a pair of shoes or play a bit of banjo in exchange for a piece of pie and a night of shut-eye in the back shed before moving on in the morning.

Smoothy knew the history of these kindred spirits well. And he was committed to their tradition, spirit and unwritten code. While I knew him for less than one full day, I learned more about hobos and rail-runners in that time than I had heard, or imagined, in my life: calculating the timing of a safe jump, how to land and tumble from a moving freight car, shimming a sliding door so it looks locked but isn't, rolling your belongings so they won't spill in a foot chase, and building smoke-free fires in small enclosures. While kids his age book-learned academic sciences, he figured out the sciences he required on his own. Rather than feeling stuck with his lot in life, he embraced it.

The rest of society would find his lifestyle disturbing. To the general population, his modus operandi would be considered somewhere between nomad, scavenger and pirate. But still, I found him more alive than most people I knew. And in some obscure way, more noble. While countless teenagers were sprawled out on couches for countless hours, watching reruns and testing out the newest mind-numbing video games, stuffing their faces with snack cakes and high-octane cola, this boy lived the breathtaking and heart-wrenching escapade of real-life survival on his own terms. Smoothy made his peril an adventure and turned his crushed young life into a storybook.

I met Smoothy beneath the long shadow of the CN Tower. There, less than two blocks west of Toronto's Union Station, is a fabulous and often overlooked memorial facing the nine parallel tracks that bleed into a wild weave entering the boarding stations. It was erected in honour of the seventeen thousand-plus workers from the province of Kwangtung (now Guangdong), China who came to Canada to work on the treacherous western section of the Canadian Pacific Railway. More than four thousand lost their lives in the process. The memorial has always had a special place in my heart and imagination because of the beautiful and tragic words on its mounted plaque. In particular, "With no means of going back to China when their labour was no longer needed, thousands drifted in near destitution along the completed track. All of them remain nameless in the history of Canada."

One of the secret joys of street work is discovering the interesting nooks and crannies of the city—the missed sites and out-of-the-way offerings only appreciated by those moving slowly. Every city has a rich history that can only be realized on foot. Small monuments and brass plaques sadly undervalued in the now, but thoughtfully set in place with tears and best intentions. One of the unexpected perks of being a street worker is having the opportunity to stumble across them, and the time to enjoy them.

As I stood beneath the wooden beams of this tall memorial, looking over the steep concrete embankment onto the tracks, the rich smell of pipe smoke washed over me. I looked from side to side, but there was no one in sight. Still, the unmistakable smell did not subside. Finally, some fifty meters to my right, I spotted a red and white bag tied to a big stick bouncing off the metal balustrade. Immediately after, a pair of white knuckles emerged, clinging to the railing. Then an elbow. Then the top of tartan cap. Every few seconds I could hear the sounds of faint grunting. Then another elbow and two scrawny shoulders appeared. And finally, with a giant thrust, he tumbled over the barrier. He had found the only place along the corridor where a person could take a running jump from the ditch and shimmy their way out of the railway yard. He stood up slowly, brushed the dust from his pants, shook off his cap, secured the pipe between his teeth with pride and, shouldering his belongings like a soldier with a rifle, he began towards me.

"Hey-ho" was the first thing out of his mouth once he reached me. While I was startled by the way he popped out of nowhere, he was nonchalant, acting as though he had been expecting me there, and without pause began rambling to me—a total stranger—about the joys of pipe smoking. Something jovial and sincere about how the calming effects far outweigh the physical consequences. He was hilarious.

After several nods, chuckles and an affirming smile, I introduced myself. He responded brightly, "And my name is Smoothy. Spelled however you like, as long as you say it kindly."

"Don't care much for the city," he went on, without hesitation. "Believe it or not, it's harder for me to fit in in a big city of three million than it is in a small town of three hundred. It ain't the numbers, y'see. Fitting in ain't about numbers."

I wrote the words on my hand, then and there, to be sure I would not forget them. *Fitting in ain't about numbers.* All my years of attending youth development conferences and special courses, and no one had said anything as profound as this young drifter in his first five minutes.

I spent the rest of the day with Smoothy. A great gift of a day, stuffed with intriguing stories, and plenty of belly laughs. We sat in the shade of two dozen pine trees, meticulously dropped in rows at the corner of Spadina Avenue and Blue Jays Way, drank grape soda and ate Ritz crackers. Picnic items compliments of Smoothy, mysteriously prearranged for today's leg of his adventure.

He could sputter out five or six run-on sentences in a row, laugh for an additional ten seconds and take a long drag from his pipe before ever needing to inhale. Every story was buttoned up with countless elbow nudges and just-between-you-and-me winks. And still, somewhere in the telling of each saga, a hint of hurt would poke its head out and duck away as though afraid of the light. His leprechaun smile and quick wit were both his defense and his offense. But wrapped tightly by a patchwork quilt of one-liners, puns and semi-famous quotes was the concealed travelogue of a boy running from a pain too great to stop and face.

When I asked his real name, he told me "Smoothy is my real name. My ma gave me a different one, but she never knew me, so it didn't stick. But some old prairie dog hobos gave me this one, glad to meet me when I showed up with tobacco, apple moonshine and a box of Fudgeos to share." He spoke as though reading from an old movie script. He never did tell me his real name. Or, for that matter, where he had originally come from.

Growing up next to train tracks in Weston, I had always had affection for the sights and sounds of the rails. I spent an entire childhood hacking around with my friends on the tracks—laying out pennies and chestnuts to be crushed, playing chicken on the overpasses and sneaking onto open boxcars. For me, the clatter of passing trains and the whistle blowing was a comforting sound. It still is. The familiar sound of being at home.

In July and August, when it was really hot and all the windows were wide open all night long, I used to lay awake and time the trains, or try to count the cars by sound. Every two clacks was a single freight car passing by the open fence at the end of the street. Three quick clacks came from each of the cars on the passenger trains. I used to drift off to sleep imagining where they might be going, who might be on them and what it would be like where they finally stopped.

As un-epic as my tales were next to his, I shared these memories with Smoothy. Surprisingly, he listened without a saying a word. Very quietly. Very intently. At first I thought he was just being kind and trying to respect my own appreciation for the adventure and imagination of locomotive travel. But when I was done talking he asked me about something in my story that had nothing at all to do with trains or tracks.

"Were they big windows?" he asked.

I was perplexed by his question. "What windows?"

"In your room," he said softly, "...the ones kept open in July and August. Were they big windows?"

"Um, well ya," I stuttered back, "the windows in my room were big, but the part that opened with the screen was kinda small." I was baffled by the strange detour in the conversation.

"Was it your room? I mean your very own room?" he dug deeper.

"Well, sort of. I shared it with my brother when I was little," I replied.

"Oh, but still, not with the furnace or the washing machine or anything, right? Just your stuff, right? Did you have your own stuff? Like, what kind of stuff?" He began to burst with strange and detailed questions, longing to hear about my childhood bedroom.

My stories of imagining train travels were lost on him the instant I mentioned having a bedroom. My room. My place of childhood belonging. A place I dreamed and wished and imagined from, like most children. A place where, most of all, I was safe.

My moment had come. "Did you have a room as a kid?"

Lost in the moment, he answered before he meant to. "Well, I guess, well, not really. A small space in the basement. No windows though. No way out until the door was unlock...." Before he finished the word, he stopped, recognizing that he was saying much more than he had ever intended.

"Never mind," he cleared his throat.

"Anyway," he continued in an about-face manner, "I sleep under the stars now. The sky is my window, and I come and go as I please."

While tragedies and atrocities occur around the world, packaged for our convenience in sound-bite morsels on the evening news, there are households in every community here at home filled with their own silent horrors. Not squabbles and struggles. Those are the property of every household and every relationship. But horrors, true horrors. The streets are filled with people, young and old, who carry the haunts of indignity, humiliation, embarrassment and abuse in the creases of their hearts and minds. It is unimaginable to most people that anyone would lock their child in the bare blackness of the basement. But still, it happens. Despite the assumption that it wouldn't happen on my street or your street, still, it happens on someone's street.

George Bernard Shaw once said, "I never thought much of the courage of the lion tamer. Inside the cage he is at least safe from people." But there are some, like Smoothy, who have had to live through terror both inside and outside of that cage.

Chapter 3

And this is why—all faith persuasions and alternative logic aside—I can only believe that God is the only hope any of us has for complete healing. Or at least as complete as possible in this lifetime. Because only he will ever know our deepest hurts and darkest secrets, and the tortures a soul has endured while on earth.

It is incredible the things most of us take for granted. Plain old things like breakfast cereal in a clean bowl, a clothing basket full of fresh laundry, a clean towel after a hot shower, framed pictures of a family holiday. Or even a small sliding window and an unlocked door. The list is endless. Things that a boy dubbed Smoothy would never take for granted, then or now.

As twilight fell and the fast and furious exchanges slowed, Smoothy dropped his guard completely. He fell asleep beneath the pines. Another gift to me—the trust that he could rest in my presence and know that he was safe. I sat at his side and thanked God for all the open windows and unlocked doors in my life. And I pleaded with God that Smoothy's path would only know such light and freedom for the rest of his days.

After an hour he awoke, as though an alarm had gone off. The sound of hitching cars linking up down below were his cue to press on. He sprang to his feet, gathered his meagre belongings and lit his pipe.

"This is my ride, friend," he nodded towards the tracks.

He shook my hand and said merrily, "Keep on fightin' the good fight!" A shock of a statement to me, as the phrase had meant so much to me that I had it tattooed on my shoulder many years prior.

I smiled sadly and responded hesitantly as he ran towards the lowest section of the easement and jumped the rail: "You too, friend."

He didn't respond, so I guessed he hadn't heard me. So I shouted it again. But he was busy working out the timing of his long strides against the side of a boxcar while it gathered momentum. Then, just as he had himself in perfect sync with the slight opening in a freight door, he turned back, winked with a giant nod, tipped his hat and called out, "At least I'll go down swinging."

He leaped. And he was gone.

I leaned back against the giant rocks at the sides of the Memorial to Commemorate the Chinese Railroad Workers in Canada. Massive nuggets of rock carved from the Rocky Mountains where the workers had toiled and transported to this place in honour of them. I felt a digging in my back, thinking it was just a rough edge in the boulder. I turned and looked. And there, mounted on one of the eight-foot chunks of mountain was a tiny plaque. Written on it in both English text and Chinese script: "One by one the walkers vanish." With only a guess at its profound meaning and the history of the words, in that moment its significance was monumental to me. One by one indeed, I have watched the walkers, runners, crawlers, hiders, seekers and Smoothys vanish.

There wasn't much time to gather up the abundant blessings of knowing Smoothy, apart from one. The one we all have the opportunity to share. The one that can come from knowing someone for a lifetime, for a season, in a chance meeting or for a few hours beside the railway tracks. The blessing bestowed on others by those, like Smoothy, who live out the priceless challenge of Mother Teresa:

"Let no one come to you without leaving them happier and better."

I was left happier. Better.

Correeen had lovely round blue eyes. They were only exposed when she dropped her guard and raised her head, which was rare. But when they were, it was like catching beams of sunlight through storm clouds.

She camped with a hodge-podge of misfits and runaways, each with their own dark story, secret glories and unique approach to survival.

Among the teenagers camping between the steel I beams beneath the Gardiner Expressway was a young man in his early twenties who loved to talk about Satan. He was new to the streets—weeks at best. New enough to maintain his commitment to pointy, waxed eyebrows and the shiny blackness of it all. He wore a long leather duster-jacket covered in pentagrams and ram's head images, and tall storm-trooper boots with wire laces. He loved to skulk among the group, evil-eyeing everyone from between strands of greased hair pressed long against the sides of his face.

He caught Correeen's cautious attention, but he never caught her off guard. She watched him, but she never feared him.

Older, louder, and still with so much to prove entering real street life, he often dominated group conversations. Inevitably, he created and orchestrated countless haunted conversations about the Order of the Trapezoid, Pythagorean Tradition and the Goat of Mendes. Tired, repetitive rants about the Nine Satanic Statements and the Nine Satanic Sins. We had more than a few ironic conversations about Satanic Statement number four ("Satan represents kindness to those who deserve it instead of love wasted on ingrates") and Satanic Sin number six ("Lack of Perspective"). Many of the young people maintaining turf along this 500-metre stretch indulged him out of sheer boredom, having passed through the this-is-so-cool stage into the how-am-I-going-to-get-by stage long, long ago.

But on occasion—usually in the darkness of post-midnight—wits were stirred and nerves were tapped in very real and frightening ways. And if I were present, the young man in black would look my way and raise his head high on his long neck like a wild animal with a carcass, assuring me that he had won the hunt that night. He eerily enjoyed my presence and the opportunity it served him to centre me out as a manifestation of naïve Christianity, a pathetic Jesus and a futile God.

Within that same group of regulars claiming squatter's rights along the muddy stretch, there was an 18-year-old who moved drugs along the Lakeshore to the tune of hundreds of dollars profit a day, every penny finding its way into his veins or up his nose that same night. And by midnight, he would turn the young Satanist's conversations into his own surreal reality, get on his feet, repeat some of things he had heard, and chase the devils, snakes and spiders in his mind around the small fire pit where everyone gathered.

Some kids would laugh nervously, others just shook their heads and rolled their eyes. One just wouldn't look. Correen would sit on her hands and look down at the fire and say nothing. Just stare into the orange sparks cracking off dried twigs, used paint sticks and fragments of misplaced construction lumber. A silent little girl, working hard to escape her unimaginable reality by gazing into the only bit of light and warmth nearby. With a tiny frame, a sweet, pain-filled face, and a gentle disposition at all times, Correen was nothing like the animated group she was in the midst of, or the dark characters that monopolized the group conversations.

I had known many of the others around the nightly circle for quite some time. It was their acceptance, built on long months of presence without pressure, that allowed me to find at least some sense of community with them. It was that same acceptance that mystified the newly arrived Satanist. And it was that same acceptance that clearly worried Correen.

Why was I there? And what did I want?

Unlike any other experience I had known on the street, the gentler or more sensitive I tried to be, the more I could sense Correen's fear of me. It wore on me for weeks. Correen was a mystery even to those she gathered with. Some of the other girls would tell me they had no idea where she was coming from or what her story was. She was an outsider among outsiders. Mousy and shy, yet she stood out so vividly in her timid presence. I had worn Correen on my heart since the moment I met her as the special one God meant to humble me most.

Cults, pimps, pushers, suicide pacts—I sat in on dozens of conversations around the circle about everything "street" and otherwise. Exchanges exposing shredded hearts and souls, and depraved dialogues nothing short of shocking. And sweet little Correen was there for every single one. Even through the most graphic telling of the Satanic Rituals of Diabolatry, she was always present, saying nothing, but never leaving.

But every time the name "Jesus" was spoken, she flinched. No matter who said it. Quite often it was the young man in black who spoke it while prophesying his disturbing interpretation of Satan's ultimate plan. But on other occasions, it would be when some of the others had had enough of his banter and would ask me questions about my faith. Or just offer up some part of their own beliefs.

Whenever I would speak she would remain as still as stone, but for the tiny spasms at even the passing mention of Jesus. Over time, it was so obvious that even our frantic friend well into his midnight high would stop and take notice.

Then one rare evening, when almost all the familiar faces were gathered, I was asked by the supposed Satanist, "How the hell can you believe in Jesus?"

And I began to answer: "Cause I think Jesus may be the only one any of us can really and fully trust and...."

Correen stood up and walked away before I even finished the sentence. Not out of sight. Just far enough that she could not hear me. In the shadows of a cement partition, she crouched on a wooden freight skid, waiting for me to finish.

I continued on, speaking through the jeers of Satan's fan and the disbelief of a young group weary of the notion that they should trust anyone, and especially not a "two-thousand-year-old lie."

In the weeks that followed, my presence and the testing of my faith became a regular event. Each night it was so, Correen would walk away, sit a ways off and wait. And every night my heart would tear in two, knowing that my words were hurting her and forcing her even further from whatever strange and thorny safety she had found among the group.

So I began to temper the issue. "Let's hear what you think is important in life," I would suggest to my young friends. Often, even the most serious starting point for some kids would end in laughable rants and teasing, and on occasion I would notice Correen smile, or even chuckle. I hoped and prayed that those hesitant grins and giggles meant she felt safe, even with me there. In the days that followed she looked up a time or two around the circle and whispered a comment to the person next to her or shook her head over something dumb said aloud. My heart warmed at every little nuance of her ease and comfort.

But the nights were getting colder and uglier as October frost forecasted the season ahead. And on a wet Friday night, with the fire barely intact in the damp mud, the young man in Pentagrams leaned into the fire, glared at me and snarled, "So where the hell is Jesus now?"

Before I could even begin to fumble a response, Correen stood up and walked away.

The mocking was quick as another young man in the group (fed up with "Devil-boy" as he was mockingly called by this point) responded, "Ya, and where is Satan? He ain't helping much either."

I walked over to Correen at the freight skid, with the voices of frustrated and cold youth at my back. I sat low on a squeegee bucket and simply said, "Why?"

I did not need to say: "Why do you stay for every other dark and disturbed conversation?" or "Why does the name 'Jesus' terrify you?" or "Why on earth are you out here?"

No. Just, "Why?"

She cleared her throat and with a soft, quivering voice offered me her "why." I was shocked. All this time pussyfooting around, and all it took was asking a one-word question.

She told me how she went to church every Sunday with her family. How her family would hold hands to say grace before every meal. That her dad would teach Sunday School and help serve communion at church. How every prayer he said—the thousands of prayers she had heard him say—would all end "in Jesus' name."

Then she told me that every night after her mom was asleep, he would sneak into her bed and quietly rape his own little girl. From age six until she walked out the door at age sixteen. A decade of torture between her father's knees after midnight. A decade of hearing him talk about Jesus in the daytime and dreading his footsteps on the squeaky hardwood floor at night.

"So, I just cannot hear that name. Not ever."

My mind could barely comprehend it. That the "name above all names" could be the spark that ignites physical, emotional and spiritual terror in a child? Where is justice? Where is mercy? Where is hope? Where is healing?

No Jesus

My mind spun in circles, aching for a profound voice to bring—to bring who knows what—to the madness, the perversion, the evil of it all.

I was frantic to find a way to say "Jesus" that she would allow. Chomping at the bit for miracle quick-fix words, I stuttered and paused. "But you see...well, you gotta look at it like this". Until finally I stopped in my own pathetic tracks, and realized how shameful my agenda was. This sacred moment—what did it require? Surely not me needing to make it feel better for me. And still that is where I went in an instant—"gotta teach her to hear it my way." As though I had any real comprehension of the magnitude of her outrageous pain. Ridiculous and selfish, and wonderful proof that my own arrogant and religious pride was more than ripe. Another lie about who Jesus really is, found in those scandalous moments of my own self-indulgence.

I stopped. With tears streaming down my cheeks, I simply promised her two things. One: that I would never say Jesus' name in front of her again. And two: that if ever she wanted, I would do my best to introduce her to the Son of God, who would never ever hurt her.

She nodded "yes" to my first promise and "no" to my second.

Jesus, Immanuel. Jesus, Healer. Jesus, Redeemer. Jesus, Saviour. Loving Jesus. Compassionate Jesus. Profound Jesus. The way, the truth and the life, Jesus. Surely the miraculous Jesus I claim does not need language to touch our hearts. All those battered times we all face when language means nothing, when Jesus is Jesus no matter what words I use or don't use.

Correen only lasted on the streets of Toronto for two or three more weeks. She did not want my help. She could barely handle my presence. She never spoke to me again. No doubt, embarrassed that she had told me too much, and reeling that I couldn't just have nothing to say. The last time I saw her she was hesitantly panhandling on a busy street, when an angry businessman stopped just long enough to call her a "lazy bitch." She just kept her head low. As though staring into the late-night fire once again. I stood to the side, weighing out what I thought was my best shot at comfort. I could see her nervously looking at me out of the corner of her eye, longing to be left alone. Snared by the presence of two men jointly representing the one who crushed her soul: a suit and tie bringing abuse and a church guy with too much to say.

Like so many, she left without notice—the same way she arrived.

Where was justice? Where was mercy? Where was hope? Where was healing? Where was Correen? I have no idea. All of them lost.

Has she ever smiled or giggled again? Will she? Can she ever trust a man again—any man? Should she? Pass by a church without shaking? Can she? Hear a prayer without crying? Without weeping? Will the words of a stumbling Christian or a homeless Satanist revisit her most?

Then I think of—no, I cling to—the wonderful story of Jesus at a gathering, when a bustling group of children were brought to see him. To laugh with him, to play with him, to be safe with him. To be children with him. The bumbling disciples interfering—no way, too busy, too important, too this, too that. But no, not Jesus. He said, "Let the little children come to me, and do not hinder them, for the kingdom of heaven belongs to such as these." (Matthew 19:14)

The kingdom belongs to children like Correen who endure unspeakable agonies. Children the ages of Correen through the decade her father undid his pants and slid into her bed. Children like Correen when she cried herself to sleep knowing her entire world was wrong, wrong, wrong. Children too scared, too uncertain, too innocent, too much a child to know what to do.

These words of Jesus are easy to rhyme off, and I have heard them babbled haphazardly from countless pulpits. But they are shocking words to dare and believe. Astounding words that speak into eternity—far, far away from the sickness, the anguish, the torturing of a body and soul. Where no Jesus will hurt her. Where no Jesus will lie to her. Where no Jesus will abandon her.

Jesus only as Jesus, no matter what words are used. Finally, where she can find wholeness. Justice. Mercy. Hope. Healing. And the promise: *For the kingdom of heaven belongs to Correen.*

July 2002

The Lake Huron region is like no other in Canada. While the world-renowned Muskokas, directly north of Toronto, have begun to unfold with small towns turning into franchised small tourist cities, the northwest regions reaching to and along beautiful Lake Huron have remained mostly unchanged.

The drive from Toronto to my father's birthplace is peppered with slow stops in sleepy towns. Single-streetlight towns that boast corner stores with worn wooden floors and metal-dome Coke signs over the doorways, quaint knick-knack and craft shops with ornate verandas, and gas stations (still called service centres) where, more often than not, a friendly ol' someone in a mesh John Deere hat will saunter out to wash your windows. Between these towns, single lane highways with dusty shoulders weave around endless acres of farmers' fields, slow-moving cattle and rusty, tin-topped barns.

As an adult, born and raised in the frantic city, even after a childhood of making this drive on every holiday weekend and school break, it still feels like plopping onto the wide rolling set of an old black-and-white television show. A world far from my own that includes time to think and breathe, much politically incorrect humour, and a Sunday afternoon routine structured around meandering to the fishing hole and back for pie on the front porch.

Chapter 5

All these years later, it looks and feels the same as it did three decades ago. Same long drive. Same tiny towns. Same yellow fields. And if I didn't know better, I would guess—same old cows.

The family holiday, and we were well on our way. As hour number two of the drive finally gave way to the "less-than-an-hour-now" promise, my heart started to bounce right along with my five-year-old son's and nine-year-old daughter's.

One hundred and eighty fidgety minutes behind the dashboard get lost when you skip the final bend on Highway 6 and head straight into the home stretch that slows at "the main drag." Over the steep hill just past the first welcoming French Fry wagon, a full kilometre from the shoreline—it appears. Sauble Beach! It is magnificent. On its easiest day—a smooth canvas sprawling into tones upon tones of blue, as deepening sandbars spread between waves. At its most dramatic—nothing less than a furious freshwater ocean that commands respect and fear. And in my heart—the happiest place of my childhood.

Eager to unload and loop back for an evening swim and ice cream, we made the "hurry up" turn down the woodsy road parallel to the beach towards Red Bay, close to where my parents' vacant cottage-home awaited us. All ours for a full week.

The chit chat quickened. Giggling and remember-whens. Best-learned driving tips gave way to watching the kids in the tipped rearview mirror as often as the open road. And with no cars in sight, the fifty-kilometres-an-hour speed limit lurched into rocket speed.

But then a hush. Front seat, back seat—a startled and unavoidable hush. Cedars and pines whistled by while our eyes and minds worked furiously to get in sync.

"Did you see–?"

"You mean–?"

"Ya, I saw–"

Stunned responses in quirky unison.

Then all at once, every head spun 180 degrees.

"What on earth!"

The dark shadows of a deep forest shielding the lowering sun made it impossible to see more than a silhouette. But like every blurred image revealed in a grocery store tabloid—he, she, it—looked exactly like Bigfoot. An outline of hair almost a metre wide, from head to waist. Body hunched, trekking in and out among the trees. It was shocking.

I stopped.

"Daddy go back. Er, no, daddy don't. I mean, I dunno. I'm scared."

Hard to tell who was saying what. But I had to see.

A long slow U-turn, into a long slow acceleration. Closer. Closer. Ten metres away, five metres away—and still as wild and unbelievable as ever.

"It's a man!" Repeated from person to person in disbelief.

We drove back to the main drag before we looped back towards our destination, leaving time for each of us to process the spectacle.

Twenty kilometres an hour. Then thirty. "Where is he?" Thirty-five. Then forty.

"He's gone."

Ahead? Behind?

"Did we pass him?"

Then, "There he is! Back towards the trees!"

Sure enough, in a steady long limp, a man like no other I have seen before or since, faded into the browns and greys of Huron tree trunks. Like Bigfoot. Just like the legend of Bigfoot.

In the days that followed we drove that road like hawks waiting on field mice. We carried bottled water and fruit, thinking maybe we could offer them to this soul lost to everything including civilization. But nothing. We asked probing questions at every quick stop in every tiny town we zipped through: at the Tim Horton's donut shop in Hepworth, at the Wiarton Willie motel and gift shop, and at the gas, lunch and bait stop in Mar, but no one could speak with any certainty. Apparently a few folks had spotted him somewhere, at some time. Every so often someone responded like an Elvis-spotter with a secret story to tell.

"Ya—I saw him. Real quick. No one believes me when I tell 'em. But I saw him."

Our days ran into each other like only summer days up north can and our week crept away on us. The daily scouting reports on the drive to and from the beach had become less and less ambitious. The morning of our last full day began with a breakfast visit from my aunts, who share a cottage around the bend, and one of their friends. The wide picnic table on the back deck was adorned with warm English muffins, sweet jams, all kinds of ripe fruit and a fresh pot of tea. The great lake in gentle ripples as a pair of loons bobbed in and out of sight. Easy, carefree catching up on the big back deck, while staring into the great blue expanse of lake and sky. Perfect.

One corner of the deck juts out past the cottage with a view of the water on one side and the gravel road on the other. With a quick glance away from the view, my wife Diane stopped. Her eyes grew huge. She looked over at me slowly.

Chapter 5

One of those "don't ask—just look" looks. And we all leaned in to see. With shuffling feet raising a small wake of dust and the morning sun wrapped around him like a blanket, it was, it was—him.

I looked at Diane. Back at him. At my aunts. Back at him. Then we all muttered the same disjointed things to one another in half sentences, all amounting to—let's invite him up to the table.

As I jumped off the stairs onto the lawn, I vividly remember my thoughts during the few seconds towards the road: "Dear God, even here? Even on vacation, at a cottage down a dirt road in obscure little Howdenvale? Even here?"

"Um, hey?" My less than brilliant intro. "Hi. Listen, we're all just right there," gesturing towards the cottage. "We have lots to eat, and we're just sitting right outside. Do you wanna come and join us?"

He was incredible. Years and years of time among homeless youth and adults, and I had never seen anyone like him. He was thin and wiry and covered in grime. His skin was like the thick, brown, cracked leather on my motorcycle saddlebags, peeling away in red tears along his nose and cheeks. And his hair! His hair was both gruesome and magnificent all at the same time. One gigantic mass, twisted and matted, as wide as his shoulders, down to his hips.

"Okay," he said kindly.

I was shocked. "Okay?" Really? I was ready to be ignored, feared, grunted at, frightened.

I was ready for silence, babbling, delusion, mental illness. I was not ready for a sane and simple "okay."

That was it though—"okay"—and we were on our way. We walked back across the lawn together. I could see the surprised bodies on the back deck rising in their seats. It was one of those inestimable moments spoken best by the old Turkish proverb: "Things never go so well that one should have no fear, and never so ill that one should have no hope."

As we sidestepped my mom's big flowerpots onto the deck stairs I asked him his name. He answered. Ryan.

Ryan. Normal, regular, know lots of them—Ryan.

"This is Ryan," I said matter-of-factly.

And everyone chimed in pleasantly, "Hello Ryan," as though we have guests we once thought were fabled half-men-half-monsters for breakfast every day.

He looked at the food spread clear across the table. Set out with care, for company. In colourful bowls, on flowered platters. All of a sudden it felt like we had ten times the food I had thought was originally there. The abundance felt embarrassing and ridiculous.

"What would you like?" Diane offered with a soft smile, stretching her arms across the table, ready to stop at any item he looked interested in.

Some of this? How about that? My aunts sweetly engaged.

Before he could answer, two fresh wee faces had woken from inside and found their way to the sliding patio doors. My children. Eyes as wide as saucers. Amazed! Jake and Sarah Jane staring at Bigfoot sitting at the picnic table. He looked back at them, smiled and nodded.

"This is Ryan," I said as gently as I could, so they would hear daddy's over-compensating calm.

Huddled close with shy smiles, quicker and freer than any adult, my kids could instantly see the gentle soul through the shocking exterior, and they joined us on the deck without hesitation.

Finally Ryan reached into the bounty and tenderly plucked two purple grapes from an overflowing bunch. He placed them in the palm of his hand and said thank you. He was a gentleman. He was peaceful. He was incredible.

He spoke with us for a while. Mid-forties, with the heart of a child and the appearance of an ancient mythological creature. Walking for months and sleeping in the bush. From Toronto to Tobermory he told us—and almost there. Through all those towns. Along all those fields. Past all those cows.

After two grapes—only two grapes—he stretched his legs and said, "Thank you, I should go now." And he stood.

But we were not satisfied. No! We had to do more! Stop him, feed him, help him—surely he needed us! Everyone must be terrified of him, but we ventured out—at last real, live people reaching out! Maybe meeting us would change everything! Turn back the hands of time, return him to civilization, where he could find—

Nope. He did not need us. In fact, by this point it almost felt like he had come to the table in the first place just to be polite. Didn't want to be rude so, as untimely as it was for him, he fit us into his schedule.

"Is there anything we can help you out with? Can we pack up some of this food? Take some bottled water? What about socks?"

We were dizzying and relentless, good-hearted and sincere, too much and too little—all at once. We offered everything but the moon and the kitchen sink to a guy who had walked hundreds of kilometres, over many months, carrying not one thing but the plastic shopping bag tied to his belt loop.

I began walking back to the road with him. Just the two of us. And just as we reached the storm ditch I noticed his shoes. Shoes that were barely shoes at all. Torn, worn, walkin'-forever shoes.

Chapter 5

"How about shoes?" I sprang to life once more. "My shoes, these shoes, these are good comfortable running shoes. Great for walking!" And he tipped his head as if to finally say, "maybe."

We both sat on the front lawn. I looked back and could see everyone on the deck watching us, trying to figure out what on earth was happening. He tried them on. Too small. I begged him to wait. My dad's feet are bigger and he had left lots of shoes there. I ran inside, then in and out of three closets, and came out with a pair of hiking boots, a pair of walking shoes, and a pair of sneakers. Too small, too small, and too small. Bigfoot? Big Feet? For a twisted moment, it was not lost on me. He thanked me for trying and was keen to be on his way.

But as he had tried them on, his own shoes were lying upside down in front of me. The soles had holes in them the size of my fist. The pain of walking those gravel roads must have been immense.

The end result? Aunt Carolyn and I sat with him on the front lawn and cut cardboard insoles out of a detergent box. And of course, we made one last plea to take a few items along the way.

Finally he was nearly free of us, our good will, our hypersensitivity and eagerness. He was leaving with a few more grapes in his plastic bag, a tuna sandwich he had to promise to eat in the next two hours before the sun made the mayonnaise toxic, a bottle of water, a pair of socks in each of his pockets—all riding on box tops from Tide.

I walked alone with him to the bulrushes that mark the end of my parents' property. He turned, smiled and shook my hand.

"Thank you," he nodded.

"But we didn't give you much," I said sheepishly as he began to walk away.

And he stopped. Stood straight. Then he turned around to face me, lifted his feet and looked at the cardboard bottoms one at a time, tapped on each one, and said—"A person doesn't need much. Just needs the right thing."

He tilted his head, winked, turned, and walked away.

I am quite certain that among his amazing secret travels I have been forgotten like so many others, quickly and assuredly. But I will not forget him. His grace. His distinction. His mystery. Or the words of a man who can grasp cardboard insoles in bottomless shoes as a blessing.

If only I could walk in his shoes.

July 2001

He delivered department store flyers for months so he could buy the small bird and the white wire cage. It was made clear that the only way he could have a pet was if he paid for it, and if it was small enough he could take care of it himself. He did. It was.

Elliot—just 14 years old. A small 14 at that. I saw him sitting there at nine o'clock in the morning, on the cracked curbside of the Bay Street bus terminal—the bus dock for passenger coaches that wander all across the nation. I was suspicious: no adults were near, and his body language told me he was carrying the weight of the world on his very young, very slight shoulders.

I spent my morning easing down the alleyways parallel to the artsy Queen Street strip, chatting with graffiti artists as they made colourful life statements on private and public property. At noon I purposefully wound my way back to the depot. Sure enough, there he was. He hadn't moved.

He was dressed in summer clothing that looked worn, but clean. Tidy, the way kids often look when raised by a mom who doesn't have much, but does her very best.

I stood off to the side, among the busy travelers, uncertain of what to do. The fear of bringing him fear imposing on every jerky step I tried to initiate. Reluctantly, I finally convinced myself just to move forward and trust God to fill in the blanks.

So I did. I sat beside him nonchalantly. Not too close, but near enough that he might guess that it was a purposeful choice.

But, what to say? "Can I help you?"... "Are you lost?"... "Are you alone?"

None of them would have been right. None of them would have been safe. All of them classic introductions made by street predators hunting for naïve and nervous girls and boys who step off out-of-town buses all alone.

I looked at him and smiled. "Hey, can I call someone for you?"

He looked up. His chin quivered and his little red eyes filled with tears. Without a moment's hesitation, he nodded eagerly, "My mom." He was simply all out of bravery. He had used it all up just to make it this far.

The lowdown was simple and sad. Mom and dad had recently divorced. Very messy. Very painful. Lots of getting hurt, and lots of giving hurt. School year with mom, summer with dad. Mom's not doing too well on her own. Dad is doing even worse.

And so, the first day of summer looked like this for Elliot:

Dad to be home at five o'clock. Dad's not home at five o'clock. Elliot waits. Six o'clock. Seven o'clock. Eight o'clock. Midnight. Waiting. Sitting at the kitchen table, whistling back at his only companion, between the vertical wires framing the small cage. The bird he had worked and saved for. Elliot wanted to show his dad two things. His new little feathered friend and his report card. A's! All A's. A very bright boy.

Finally dad stumbled in, drunk and angry. Yet somehow one tiny sound reigned over the slamming of doors, slurred curses and a little boy trying to vanish. Repeating semitones from a little cage, Elliot's wee bird was just too loud—"too damn loud." And a frightened boy, who should have been dreaming of all the fun things a young boy dreams about the day school lets out for the summer, watched his sloppy, raging dad reach into the small white cage on the kitchen table, take out the chirping bird, and crush it in his large dirty hands.

Elliot sheepishly told me his phone number back "home." Home—where mom is.

And I called mom. "Elliot is here. He has been here since shortly after midnight."

Mom was in rough shape, but clearly she loved her little boy. Her only dear child. Besides the desperation and sorrow in mom's voice, it was filled with love and embarrassment. Mom and I worked it out—a good plan, a simple plan, a trusting plan on everyone's part. One that found Elliot on the next bus home. Mom's home. Mom's safe and loving home. "For good!" I was told. Who knows? Still, it was one life the street did not steal that day.

A Lucky Bird

Time and time again, this is how it goes. There is always that final thing—sometimes big, sometimes small, always deep and weighty—that forces a tender heart and young mind to unite and be decisive that this is the time to run. One night on the streets is always proof that a second night is not impossible. And that's proof that a third isn't. You meet other kids who understand your pain. Kids, it seems, who are there for all the same reasons as you, born out of the cutting and ugly details uniquely their own. You stay. The street wins. Hundreds and thousands of them as minutes become days, days are lost into seasons, and seasons are churned into years.

But not on this day! On this day there was just enough time for a street vendor's meal and a quick chat before Elliot's bus came and went. I told him who I was, and he told me who he was. A good talk. A safe talk. Safe, only because Elliot had already heard his own mom's promising and loving voice telling him it was so.

His bus pulled up and stopped with a jolt. The coach doors opened with a dramatic hydraulic gasp. But each small step in the boarding line carried the hesitation of something still left to say. And then, a boy struggling to understand the ridiculous nuances of love and fear spun around with a question in the final moments.

"Will my bird go to heaven?"

His eyes widened and shoulders curled in, waiting in anticipation for the answer he longed to hear.

As wishy-washy as it may seem, it is in times like these that one leans into the theology of those who say what you want to hear: the likes of Albert Schweitzer, Martin Luther, John Wesley, Pope John Paul II, and of course St. Francis of Assisi. All supporters of the belief that animals have both souls and a place in heaven.

The hopeful quiver in his cracking voice owned me. "Yes, I think so," I answered, truly believing with all of my heart that if even just one bird from earth gets there, surely this has got to be the one.

The simple answer found the centre of Elliot's heart, and while holding the line at a standstill, he shocked me. He carefully reached into the pocket of his khaki shorts. Elliot pulled out a red and white bandana, rolled neatly into a tight ball, and handed it to me gently. I stepped towards him and unfolded the corners. Inside was the quiet body of a tiny blue and yellow bird.

"Will you bury him somewhere nice?" he whispered.

Tears welled up in my eyes as I fought to keep a confident smile in honour of Elliot's remarkable courage. I nodded.

Chapter 6

"Yes. Yes, I will," I promised.

Less than a kilometre east of the playful greens of Sunnyside Park, just off the boardwalk that curves along the shoreline facing Toronto's famous skyline, and beneath a blanket of smooth white stones are the remains of a beautiful tiny bird. A bird that will never be forgotten. An innocent bird. Peaceful. So very special. Once loved, and forever remembered. A lucky bird! A lucky bird to have been cherished by a boy blessed with the courage to live, love and hope against all odds.

Hope is the thing with feathers
That perches in the soul.
And sings the tune
Without words
And never stops at all.

— Emily Dickinson

Dancing over hell? Or earth turned hell? Or post-apocalyptic rubble? Whatever. Didn't really matter to me—it was fascinating!

I was eleven years old, hiding under a coffee table at my aunt and uncle's farmhouse, and I just couldn't take my eyes off it. Four men in platform boots and kabuki makeup, heroic above the fire and brimstone. Ken Kelly's legendary cover for the KISS album, *Destroyer*.

It was my older cousin's newest purchase. A just-released album that went on to devour the mid-seventies music scene. At the time, I had not heard one note of the music, and I didn't care. It didn't matter what they would or wouldn't sound like. I was an instant fan because of one single image. Light years away from the flannel graph Bible character cutouts I grew up on as a boy in Sunday School. Worlds away from the images I was allowed to pin on my bedroom wall or wear on a t-shirt at that age. But something about it secretly made me want to be a part of it all. I still wanted mom to be mommy some days, and dad to be daddy on others, and to have my favourite cereal while watching Saturday morning cartoons. Ten and eleven are tricky ages, filled with wanting to grow up and not wanting to at the same time. But with this picture, some prepubescent Dr. Jekyll and Mr. Hyde nerve was touched, and the preteen in me wanted very much to belong in the unreal and spooky world of KISS.

Knowing where we belong is the challenge of a lifetime. As it turns out, I didn't belong dancing over hell. Just close enough to smile sympathetically and bob my head to the beat.

But two decades after the country coffee table incident, this was all brand new. I was long past feeling like a stranger in the world of shock-rock. I was not used to being an outcast among street-involved young people who considered themselves outcasts. Like anyone, there have been countless times and places that my own insecurities and quirky comfort levels have made me feel "I don't belong." The older I get, the less it seems to matter to me, apart from the times I end up milling about in the unsocial corners of places I don't want to be. Formal functions, high-end corporate events, fancy parties, and extra-churchy things. But never among young people with tattooed sleeves and multiple piercings. I have always felt at peace among those from any of the dozens of underground street subcultures.

But there I was. Sitting with a friend in the back row of a historic Toronto sports arena nearing the end of its rope, fearful that I was at the end of mine.

Marilyn Manson's startling album *Anti-Christ Superstar* hit Toronto with the same force it hit most major North American cities in 1996. A shock-rock phenomenon, debuting at number three on the Billboard charts. The Goth movement had been flowing beneath the rock-and-roll landscape like a cold current under ice for many years. But this album broke through that ice like a panicked whale and opened a hole wide enough for Goths, subculture outcasts, teenage vampires and witches, young people with dark fascinations, wounded adolescents, confused youth and mainstreamers all to dive into. And all at once.

Several of the newer young people I was meeting on the streets were quite stirred with Manson, his music and his message. I had heard his most recent release *Smells Like Children* in passing, but to really know well the substance of the new *Superstar* album, I bought it. It opens with a live version of the song "Irresponsible Hate Anthem" and ends with the song "Man That You Fear" in which he sings, "The world is in my hands, there's no one left to hear you scream/There's no one left for you." A chaotic, hateful, hopeless collection of surrealistic songs.

Born Brian Warner in Canton, Ohio, Manson grew up to become one of rock-and-roll's ultimate antiheroes, was ordained into the First Church of Satan and claimed in a *Spin* magazine interview: "I always wanted to become what adults feared most." For a while, he was.

And the truth is—while the lyrics, images and messages felt wicked to the core, full of unhealthy terror and drenched in untruths and theology completely counter to my faith—I actually found the music, in and of itself, interesting and intriguing. The industrial samples woven into the abrupt live performances, the innovative layers of vocals, voices and effects in wide ranges of pitch, and the bombastic sonic tenor alone were collectively groundbreaking.

Especially in the mainstream. It sounded urgent. Ferocious and relentless. Something with an undeniable reach, heavy with adrenalin hooks, and the riff for the hit single "The Beautiful People" went on to become a staple in most sports arenas as an aggressive backdrop for player introductions.

Still, at the back of an outdated sports centre filled with wound-up Manson disciples a year after the album's wildfire release, no one cared about my appreciation for the evolution of sound. I represented the enemy. And while there were certain moments of fear, the sickness I felt most was sadness.

MuchMusic, "the nation's music station," was working through the initial blueprint for an hour-long feature they wanted to produce. This national broadcast on what was, at the time, Canada's MTV equivalent was to be called *Too Much for Much*. The premise was to explore the current music and musicians who were creating a buzz by stretching the limits of what the elastic mainstream—censors, parents, and religious-types—would allow. A concept reborn repeatedly in one form or another at every turn in rock-and-roll history, dating back to the early days when Sun Studio first rolled tape in Memphis. I received a call from a television producer who had been searching for a youth worker who worked among "street-types," as he called them, with some knowledge of rock music. The fact that I had been playing in a hard rock band for years made me even more intriguing. But that I answered "yes" to his question, "Would you say you are a Christian?" put me on the top of the producer's list. We spoke for some time as he laid out the working ideas for the panel-style show and convinced me to be a part of it.

Soon after MuchMusic's phone call, the live broadcast date was upon me. The panel guests assembled in a green room, where we were reminded why each of us had been invited. Even as we departed the green room, we were coached through the hallways one more time: "It's live. It's nation-wide. Remember this is live. Jump in. Be aggressive. People have their hands on the converters. Remember why you were asked to be part of this." It was like being on a high school football team heading towards the gridiron for the dramatic championship game. Go team go!

The dimly lit studio was filled with teenagers and young adults. A multitude of the band's fans in white, pasty makeup and shoe polish hair dye were joined by a skittish minority of quasi-fans and non-fans. After the panelists were miked and seated in a circle in front of the audience, Reverend Manson walked in, shouldered by a bodyguard who did not leave his side through the entire broadcast. The room was electric with fans calling out and cheering for their dark hero.

Chapter 7

Once on air, I was the fourth to be introduced, between a newspaper jour-
nalist and a young man introduced as a "recovering Goth." My heart sank as the
host introduced me: "Word is that he is a Christian, but don't be afraid." I had
anticipated the dynamic they were looking for, but I was sadly taken aback by
the sense that I was there to represent a counter-evil in the eyes of evil.

Manson was as clever and unflappable as his reputation boasted. He chose
his words carefully as he spoke about young people who followed his lead in
self-mutilation. The crowd cheered during an exchange with me when he said,
"Your only salvation is in yourself." He was abundantly calm and collected, the
opposite of his stage and video persona.

The hour passed with a strange heaviness, more bleak than oppressive.
While the cameras were on, I forced myself to stay focused on the conversation.
There were two girls—no more than 13 or 14 years old—sitting just outside the
glare of the stage lights. They were dressed in witches' garb, with shiny black
bustiers wrapped awkwardly around their tiny adolescent frames. They had
charcoal smeared across their eyelids and black x's painted on their foreheads.
Two wee girls huddled close together, heads darting back and forth to see what
the popular response was to every word and movement Manson made. They
would look around and giggle or cheer when they saw everyone else doing it. Or
scowl and boo just after they saw and heard that others were. Just little girls,
imitating a darkness they had no comprehension of. I imagined their conversation on the way home: "What about that stupid Christian guy." My mind
began to race. What could I say to make sure they knew God was not the enemy?
That God loved their searching young hearts, and wanted to bring peace to
their nervous little souls, even as they played with a black magic fiercer than
they understood. Even if no one else in the room caught it, what could I say to
them?

The panel also included a poet/writer and a professor/philosopher. Deep
thinkers and wordsmiths. While the dialogue rose to headier babble and more
self-indulgent interpretation by the minute, all I could think about were those
two little girls. The ones who didn't seem to really understand what everybody
was saying, but pretended they did, even while trying to figure out how to
sneak back into their homes without their parents seeing them.

In a final on-air exchange, I offered my concern for young people who didn't
understand the difference between the disturbing metaphors and reality. My
hope was that two girls, just a decade older than my own daughter, would hear
that and wonder about it. But the man of the hour was on. "I can appreciate
where you're coming from," he said. "We're not that far apart." And I lost. In

fact, it was such a surprise response that I felt flustered. As the show rolled to credits, Manson looked at me and smiled.

A producer's quick pat on the back and a brief (and pleasant) hallway conversation with Manson later, and I was out the front door. All along the Queen Street entrance, eager fans waited for Marilyn Manson to resurface. I snaked through the crowd while agitated fans stirred around me, sneering and giggling at me through rings of cigarette and pot smoke.

My friends, family and co-workers were proud and encouraging in the days that followed. I was a "voice of reason," one very churchy friend told me. It didn't help. In fact, inexplicably, it made me feel even worse.

I was hurt. I felt betrayed. I felt sad. Behind the glued hair and graveyard wardrobes were young people who feel the same things we all do. Sad, happy, wishful, nervous. I had always known a sense of community with people living their lives at street level because we met at common places in our humanity—not by building up walls with our differences. And while I was surprised and felt sucker-punched by Manson's statement about us not being so different, there was actually some disturbing and pleasing resonance in that for me.

The broadcast aired several times throughout the week. A short time later, I was three provinces west of my own, at a McDonald's in Calgary, when two Goth-looking kids sauntered up and said, "We know you! You're that guy on Much, who just doesn't get it!"

I felt sick. Again, hurt. Again, betrayed. Again, very sad.

*Sticking it to the man...embracing the counter-culture...exposing the pain and the pain-makers...peeling back the layers of a corrupt and unjust society by displaying the grotesque truth...seeking the spiritual apocalypse by choosing hate over love, and Satan as self...blah, blah, blah...*or even just naïvely dunking one's young self in the latest trend for the current rock-and-roll rebel—whatever it was, whatever it is, whatever hardcore verbiage paints the picture best, I did get it. For most teenagers, what they see in the mirror comprises nine-tenths of their identity. But the mirror always lies because it can only reveal an image, a shell. Not a soul. And these souls were tortured, fed up, searching, or simply playing with fire. Behind all the darkness, horror and confusion there are souls. Young people angry with God. Young people searching heaven and hell for truth. Young people with a fresh antihero willing to invite them into a new identity where grotesque things are beautiful and beautiful things are ridiculous. Some believed it. Some nailed themselves to it. And some scuffed their knees getting on and off the bandwagon. Still, every single one—a soul. I got it. I get it.

Chapter 7

Just six months after the MuchMusic broadcast, Manson—man and band—returned to Toronto. Thursday, July 31st, 1997, Varsity Arena, at the corner of Bloor and Bedford.

By now the music video for the song "The Beautiful People" was legendary for its disturbing, nightmarish and impressive visuals. I was eager to check the whole thing out live. I wanted to see and hear it for myself. One of the constant (and often legitimate) criticisms of Christians, parents, and grown-ups in general is that they speak of things they know nothing about. So my friend Paul (Youth Unlimited's Youth Culture Specialist) and I purchased tickets.

It was a hot summer evening. Paul came in golf shorts and sandals. I felt safer and much more "in" wearing my ripped jeans and a ragged t-shirt. But I was no further ahead. The street was flooded with what looked like extras from *The Rocky Horror Picture Show*. Coincidentally, we greeted each other right in front of a group of religious protestors. Signs calling for repentance. Placards with random scriptures from the book of Revelation. A woman carrying a huge framed oil painting of Jesus. And street preachers preaching.

While Paul and I exchanged "wows" around the explosive buzz, three hyped-up Manson fans crawled into my personal space like bugs.

Spitting into my face, "You're that guy! From that show!"

They were disgusted. Seething. One was literally growling. Paul and I couldn't believe it. More than eight months had passed. I had played a small role in a one-off taping. We just couldn't believe I was identified, or that anyone cared.

They were dressed to the nines in industrial concert wear, with lazy Alice Cooper makeup melting around their eyes in the summer heat. I looked at Paul and shrugged in bewilderment. Then I looked slowly over my shoulder: Street preacher. Standard Jesus-looked-like-this painting. Turn-or-burn signs. I thought, OH NO!...they think we're part of the religious protest!

In the blink of an eye, I reached inside my pocket. A ticket! My own Marilyn Manson concert ticket. Section J. Row N. Seat 4. I held it up, spun it at eye level, and nodded as if to say, "Surprise! You got the wrong guy!"

They were not convinced, but were thrown by the ticket all the same. Paul and I reluctantly wandered to the line. We couldn't have looked more out of place if we had tried.

The line went as far as the eye could see and swayed back and forth with vinyl and leathered bodies shoving one another in heated anticipation. Inch by inch we moved towards the ticket-takers. Every so often someone stumbling out of line would notice me, do a double-take and scowl. Every few minutes someone would break the line and approach us, or call out from a distance. It was shocking. I had heard that the panel show had been replayed on occasion, but I hadn't seen it—and even still, so what?

Security was extra tight. The local news had hyped the show and the crowd it drew, so every person through the wicket was frisked before proceeding. Fold-out tables were piled with confiscated flasks, bottles, pipes, cutting shanks and riding crops—rock-and-roll concert staples—as well as an obscure assortment of paraphernalia, bondage apparatus and prosthetics.

It seemed to take forever to get through the line. By the time we reached our back row seats in the arena, my body temperature had risen several degrees from the stress of being accosted, pressed and cursed at by literally dozens of aggressive concertgoers.

I knew plenty of kids on the street who claimed to be big Manson fans, but not one of them made the show. They were all homeless. The $35.25 ticket might as well have been a thousand dollars. Most just did not have it. And even for the few that did, the popular reach did not go far enough to yield the surrender of hard-earned funds, regardless of where they came from. So, while I felt I was among a desperate group, I suspected that most would still be crawling into their own beds that night.

The house lights were fully on while fans trickled in. The P.A. was barely audible with background techno-metal music. Very uncommon anti-hype procedures for a rock concert of any kind. The rabid fans were hopped up enough. It was clear the venue management did not want to ramp up the mayhem. For the first time in over an hour, I finally felt safe. Paul was relieved too. The floors were wide open and seatless—a stand-up version of what is generally called "festival seating" that allows hardcore fans to get close to the stage on a first-come first-served basis. It also gives way for the furious audience activities of impromptu slam-dancing in what's known as a mosh pit. But mainly, the whole set-up is simply a cash grab for the venue. Chairs take up more room than vertical bodies, thus more people can be squeezed in. More people equals more cash—and safety be damned.

The start time had long since passed. A buzz began on the floor about ten bodies from the front of the stage. Shouting and shoving. A small space opened up among the crowd. It grew wider and wider, and people began to cheer. Soon enough, with the bright white house lights up full, the floor audience had created an impromptu performance circle. Standing in the centre was a young man with no shirt. Toned, sweaty, drunk and loud. He cursed and laughed and did back flips while people cheered him on. "Manson! Satan! Manson!" he shouted. He laughed as though possessed and continued to do incredible back flips from a complete standstill.

After about five minutes of non-stop acrobatics, cursing and chanting, he fell to his knees and froze. And as though he was channeled from outer space, he looked straight up at me—all the way up to my back row seat. He stood slowly, pointed up at me and began shouting: "He's a Christian!" Then he laughed like a demon and shouted all sorts of things at me. It was incredible! Through the frenzied crowd, through his inebriation, through his manic delirium, from the centre of the floor to the back row, he caught sight of someone he did not want there. Me.

Sometimes one uses the expression "my jaw dropped open" to describe figuratively their astonishment. But quite literally, my jaw dropped open. I could feel it hanging there, paralyzed with disbelief. Every person in the concert bowl turned and stared at me. Jeers from the faithful came from all around us. And the body temperature at Seat 4, Row N, Section J, rose again to new heights.

The verbal abuse finally gave way to literal darkness as the lights went down and the show began. An incredible display of underworld theatrics and imagery. Hell's own revival service and an audience willing to buy into each and every word sung, squealed and preached.

"Dear God," I prayed in my head. I could not even find words or thoughts to finish the prayerful sentence. Just over and over, "Dear God." So much for dancing over hell. These moments were made for a mad dash *through* hell. Between songs, the hypnotic frontman would preach about the vital necessity for a collective disbelief in Christianity, and wired fans sitting around us would turn, point and cackle. I kept wondering if the two young teenaged girls from the television show eight months earlier were there. I prayed they weren't—that enough time had passed in their young lives that they had meandered into another safer scene. And still, even two rows in front of us, a young mom had brought her son. He was no older than ten. Just a bit younger than I had been under the coffee table. With lots more in front of him than an album cover.

Paul and I left after the final song, with the house lights still down, before the encore. Having been to hundreds of rock concerts, I had never left before the encore. But we had had a stressful enough time getting in. We couldn't imagine that this wired-for-death crowd would let us off the hook getting out.

The following day I brought lunch to one of the young homeless Manson fans I knew. He went by "Wolf" on the street. He had lacquered hair with frosted green tips, tarnished rings in his lips and eyebrows, and another thick one through his nose like a bull. I had promised him that I would meet him in a specific alleyway in the southwest end of the downtown core to tell him all about the concert. I gave him all the gory details and he listened intently. But even in the telling, I couldn't shake the sadness. And he noticed.

"What's your problem?" he sneered.

I spoke about the upset of being misunderstood. Of being judged to be something I wasn't. Of being vilified for believing something different. Of wanting to somehow belong even though I was so very different. Of being judged for the way I looked. I tried to explain it to him, and he just laughed. I thought his laughter was dismissal and the sure sign that he just could not understand.

Could there be a bigger fool than I? Of course he understood.

We sat in the quiet laneway and ate chicken subs. I was withdrawn and quiet, feeling sorry for myself. He would take a bite, then look at me and laugh. Then take another bite, look at me and laugh again.

"What's the big deal? Who cares?" he snorted.

"I know, I know." I just nodded, unconvincingly.

But I did care. I wanted to think it was for all the right reasons. I am confident it was for some of the right reasons. But there was something more—something not good. It was pride.

Thomas Jefferson once said, "Pride costs more than hunger, thirst and cold." No words could be more perfect for this scenario: a pouting man wanting to be liked by everyone, looking for validation from a homeless teenager. Pride is a ridiculous beast.

Soon enough Wolf stopped laughing and just looked sideways at me between bites. And without notice, our unscripted roles were completely reversed. He was the caregiver and comforter. And I was the discouraged outcast whose best was just not good enough.

He took his last bite, rolled up the wax wrapper and stood up.

"Listen. They just don't know who you are—but I do." He smiled kindly. Then he turned and walked away. And the weight was lifted.

He walked away to homelessness, houselessness, and a future that was hard to forecast beyond nightfall. But not before he took care of me—and my ego.

How many times had I said the very same thing to my friends on the street? "They just don't know you—but I do." A hundred times? A thousand? But I had always wandered off afterwards to my safe home, my warm bed, or a hot meal. And not once had I ever affirmed one's value because they were acting sucky.

In that moment, Wolf was a better man than I.

Chapter 7

The Goth-rockers who strangely bothered to take notice of me, from the Atlantic to the Pacific, from a Queen Street studio to a Bloor Street arena, had no idea who I really was. But Wolf did. The good, the bad and the ugly. We had spent more than enough time together working through his dark history between Ontario and the prairies, digging up legal I.D. and hunting for life options. Wolf knew me well. And in a matter of seconds, cleared my vision. Where pastors and parishioners might have failed. Where friends and co-workers could not succeed. Not in the stillness of a church pew. Not in a counselor's office. Not in the comfort of my own living room.

No. In a back alley with a boy who looked like he danced over hell daily. A boy who had already run the gauntlet though his own hell. A boy with a few choice words and a timely smile just for me and my sad and arrogant heart.

I am a great believer in the dignity found in a birth name. I feel sick when young ones on the street get tagged, or tag themselves, with ugly and painful street monikers. But, there is something very special when a young person takes on a street name that really works. He once told me that he chose the name "Wolf" in honour of his mother's First Nations heritage. He had journeyed far from that world, physically and socially. But emotionally and spiritually, the day he explained it and spoke about his mother, I knew where his true heart was.

Among the many symbolic virtues of a wolf in First Nations circles are leadership and intelligence. Wildlife experts say that wolves are among the most misunderstood animals in all of the wilderness; while a wolf may look fierce, it is actually a very emotional, non-confrontational and social creature.

All of those things added up when it came to this boy. But on this day, one more symbolic truth was even greater. A wolf has the capacity to howl—to speak—in many different tones. To show deep disturbance with one howl, joy with another. To call out caution, engagement and grief—each with its own identifiable howl. And a strong wolf is never afraid to set another one straight—to put another in its rightful place. The one thing that all wilderness authorities and experts agree on is this: Every time a wolf speaks it is extraordinary and with purpose.

Wolf spoke.

"I dunno, looks like a bunch of winos and bums getting free food and spoiling the place for everyone. The city should put an end to this kind of s**t!"

I didn't hear the question asked by the distressed thirty-something woman. But I did hear the answer from the buttoned-down man holding her hand, as they marched past me.

On a bright crisp afternoon in September, the echoes of a Marshall amp and the smell of fresh corn found their way to an unlikely crowd in an unlikely place once again. The fifth annual "Concert and Cornroast" in Allen Gardens.

It is a somewhat obscure event, designed and hosted by two partnering agencies over the years: Youth Unlimited's Light Patrol—the outreach that I am the director of—and Sanctuary—a downtown community-based ministry among street-involved people. A day simply to share with those on the street and from the street, and to remind them that they are special, vital, and indeed, our dear friends. A bit of time off the grey pavement and on the green grass, all together. No cost. No agenda. Nothing more than a time to be, enjoy, sing along, and for a few, to stumble merrily into the large fountain that rises and falls next to the ground-level stage. As always, a wild and wonderful collection of friends and characters gathered. Some new, some old. Some vertical, some horizontal, and some defying gravity on a sustained unworldly tilt halfway in between. A remarkable family of unheralded survivors.

The bands for the gig were Outrider, the band I front, and Red Rain, fronted by Greg Paul, Executive Director of Sanctuary, both gladly serving up classic rock and blues staples that bounced around the skyscrapers for blocks.

Allen Gardens is a unique park, squared off by four major intersections. It islands several blocks amid the inner city with an identity all its own. On a sunny Saturday it boasts wide-eyed touristy families enjoying popcorn and ice cream around its perimeter, hardcore skateboarders grinding along the concrete platforms at the greenhouses' entranceways, dogs chasing Frisbees along the long north extension, and scattered benches throughout the park make-shifting as gurneys for the shirtless survivors of weeklong binges and hangovers.

Each year, this particular Saturday also draws special attention from curious passersby and dispatched mounted police, hearing guitar vibrato harmonizing with the rumble of dozens of massive motorcycles. The A.B.A.T.E. motorcycle group, in full leathers, roll in each year to prepare and serve the corn and refreshments. Between the rock-and-roll at full volume, tattooed bikers lining up their scoots and hogs in a row, billowing steam from large boiling pots, and a field full of hovering street friends—the day has a vibe uniquely its own.

Although a handful of street youth will inevitably find their way to the park to eat their fill and take in the sounds, the event has always maintained a peculiar ease and pace that predominantly and consistently draws homeless adults. A weathered and hardcore street crowd keen to enjoy the last taste of summer, just before hints of the harsh seasons ahead appear. An unassuming congregation to say the least. A flock of unlikelies, embracing the fellowship of shared food and song, words of encouragement, and the soft remembrance of "welcome" and Shalom.

Each year, one ambitious old codger tries to engage me in conversation at the oddest of times. My best guess: off-the-streets appearance would gauge him somewhere well into the seventy year mark. Taking into account the unforgiving wear of the streets, perhaps early to mid sixties? Hard to say, but it was clear that he'd seen more than his unfair share of hard years. He finds his way to the side of the P.A. system while my band is playing, to engage in mumbly chats with me during guitar solos and between songs.

Three years in a row, the only time I ever saw him was in this park and on this day. And each time, he was determined to have me believe him as he told me that he was one of the original drummers for the band "Buffalo Springfield," before they hit it big in 1966 along Los Angeles's Sunset Strip. (The band, infamous to this day for its anti-establishment hit "For What Its Worth," broke up in 1968.) So thin and frail, and quite hard to understand, it was easy to guess that his story was make-believe. The cost of old age, a hint of mental unrest and long-term liquor use all likely contributing to the fantasy.

Sure enough, he was present again this year, but this time in a wheelchair, with a right leg that he had broken in a nearby harm-reduction centre where he was staying.

He made his way up to the roaring monitors and called over to me, "Remember me? I was in Buffalo Springfield. I'm Buffalo Hal—that's what they call me. Buffalo Hal." And once again he tossed it out—his wishful offer to sit in with the band.

The crowd was happy for the warm sun, the fresh food and music they recognized from eras gone by. The park was more their home than ours. And on this easy afternoon, time was on our side. So I promised him that when we were finished our set we would let him jam with us.

As we finished our set, Buffalo Hal wheeled his way towards the wedge monitors gating the front of the drum kit. The band awkwardly surrounded him to help, looking for a way to pluck him up from one side of the equipment maze and plop him down on the other. But he wouldn't have it. Excitedly, he hobbled through the cords and beneath the boom-stands on his own. He sat hunched on the stool: low and small behind the high toms. His foam baseball cap shadowed his deep-set eyes and sunken cheeks. But within seconds, his eyes were wide with wild anticipation. A sly crooked smile crossed his face. One belonging to someone quite familiar with this seat. He bounced the sticks in his hands as though he was weighing them—high-hat hand with a standard rock grip, snare-hand with a classic jazz grip. Early signs, before a single strike, that he knew what he was doing.

My band buddies led into a classic Neil Young tune, and instantly, from the first flam, he was on. Very on. Then they rolled over into some time-tested classic blues riffs, while I sang some silly spontaneous vocals about "Buffalo Hal, back on his throne." He was grooving. Eight beat fills. Punctuated snare cracks. Easy ride beats. And a park filled with alleyway companions and startled strangers stopped mid-bite, mid-sentence and mid-step to listen to the wee man behind the skins.

Our plot at the northwest corner of the park was all smiles. The volunteer bikers, the rum drinkers coming in from behind the greenhouses, the nervous dog walkers. Everyone smiling. The biggest smile of all, of course, was gleaming from four inches below a wide crash cymbal. A man who, for a few wonderful moments, told us a bit of his story with tempo, technique and timing.

Chapter 8

Did he play in Buffalo Springfield, somewhere in his hippie youth? Has he really been on Neil Young's guest list for the past twenty-five years, whenever Neil is in town? He told me so. I have no proof. Likewise, I have no reason not to believe him. In fact, I am glad to believe him and not look any further into resolving the truth.

I know this for sure. As he flopped back into his wheelchair, he was wiping the tears from his eyes, mumbling, "Thank you. Thank you. Thank you so much." On this day he was not simply an old, wobbly homeless guy to ignore, fear or pity. Not a bum or wino "getting free food and spoiling the place for everyone." For a few minutes, by providing rhythm in the warm breeze, he allowed us all to peek at one page of a story filled with the dreams and wishes of a long and interesting life. A bit of precious storytelling without words, among a circle of souls—each with their countless untold stories of splendor and heartbreak. In fact, if you ask me, on this fine day, he was holding down the fort with class for a road band, in a down-and-dirty revival beneath the metropolitan sun.

And me? Perhaps I was jamming with a withering old gent that still has some chops from an unheard-of bar band from many cloudy decades ago? But maybe, just maybe, his story was fact, and not fiction as I had assumed.

Either way...without a doubt, I was jamming with one of the greats.

December 2003

For a long time, the shoreline along the west-central bend of the Don River had a reputation for hiding many of Toronto's heaviest heroin users doing their best to survive—or die a slow death. Hidden in the snowy thickets that shield the riverbank, Tara was a week shy of her seventeenth birthday the morning after she lost her boots.

The face of any addiction, for any person, has more than one story. Addictions are volumes. Stories upon stories all belonging to one person, spilling in and out of the lives and histories of countless others. Haunting stories, shame-filled stories, toxic stories, complex stories relived, and many more forgotten. But somewhere in one of the early chapters—at the start of the whole tragic mess—there is always the mention of a line drawn in the sand. Not always descriptive. More often than not, fuzzy verbiage at best. But there all the same. It is the untidy telling of a line crossed, where the ugly trolls of addiction are no longer waiting for you. They are welcoming you.

That line was not at all blurry for Tara. Her dad introduced her to the lethal demons of cocaine and heroin at age ten, tying her off and tapping for wee veins with his own hands, in the middle of one of his own sustained crazes. He dragged her across that line in the sand with his own vile grip. Tara's entire young life story had her auditioning for no other role than victim. Until one day, in the middle of her thirteenth year, in an attempt to save her own tortured life, she made the streets her home.

Several seasons into the abuses of street life, Tara had chosen to exist alone—a rare and bold choice among teenage girls living out street life. A very bold choice. The more common choice would be to stake out an existence nearer to the sad but safer commonplace of youth in street culture found nightly in the corners of dimly lit parks and green-spaces. But from the moment she left her dreadful home, Tara had been marked by doggedness and an unyielding courage. So, in a dangerous but quiet stretch along the river that offers a blurry resemblance to a twisted Huck Finn lifestyle, Tara was one of very few women, young or old, to choose it. And the only one I have ever known to choose it alone.

Until the previous winter, her young body and pretty face had paid the way for her lonely survival. Routinely sold to her dad's perverse buddies for habit fixes, Tara knew the darkest side of too many men's existence early and often. She brought that knowledge and numbness with her to the streets, and went on to sell her body and soul on the outskirts of one the city's most notorious low-track sex work districts. There, she could sell sex wearing ripped track pants to nervous men in minivans, buy a sandwich and a pack of smokes with the fast cash, and maybe still have enough for a bagel in the morning.

But that same winter, February was ferocious, with ceaseless north winds in the downtown core, blasting in from Lake Ontario. Record cold temperatures seized the city and tormented the province. And brave little Tara fought back. Daytime hunting for firewood and burnables, evenings bent beneath the warm dashboards in strangers' cars, and back by midnight leaning into the coals just outside her shanty. The agonizing fight against a Canadian winter married to a ludicrous existence, soldiered by the tenacity of youth.

But the cold just kept getting colder. Finally, on the most bitter of all nights, with not much fight left to give, she built a small fire right inside her make-shift shelter, and fed it twigs into the wee hours. But fatigue and fire are cruel bedfellows, and Tara burned the entire left side of her sweet face.

The seasons that followed aged her rapidly. The street always forces the aging process at least two-fold. But Tara was living the hardcore day-to-day that deals an extra measure of physical, emotional, mental and spiritual cruelty. Flames robbed her of her looks, and time was stealing her drive. She'd hit the streets with little more than these in her back pocket to begin with.

Dynamite

Ten months later, during an early December freeze, I wandered past her hideaway. The long white burn scars tattooing her chin and cheeks were even more pronounced against her cold red face. Bundled tightly in an old grey army blanket, she shook uncontrollably. Before I could surrender any kind of feeble greeting, she called out to me. Her voice was deep and throaty, like an old woman's.

"It's my feet! It's my feet!" she chattered.

They were hidden beneath the stiff dark wrap. I bent down in front of her. Slowly she poked out her left foot, then her right. Two worn work boots. Men's work boots. Brown and beaten, with steel toes poking through the cracked leather. At least four of five sizes too big. Her tiny feet freezer-burned inside of them.

She tapped the steel toes together and winced. Speaking in spurts and lulls into the rhythm of the intense wind, she told me what had happened the night before.

In a back alley, an anxious first-timer literally kicked her out of his car before he did up his pants and before she could get her boots on. She barefooted her way along Parliament Street, found another homeless girl and bartered, spending the short night's earnings on a second-hand pair of Nikes. She hiked back and worked at her fire.

Some time later, as she was cursing the wet wood, an old homeless man who camped on higher ground wandered by and saw her suffering in the cold, with only tattered running shoes on her feet. As she told it, he gave her his boots, smiled and literally walked away in his sock feet—without saying a word.

After telling her tale, she looked down at her feet. Then back at me. Then down to her feet again, and she began to cry. The story of the old man's kindness was incredible. The lump in my throat made it hard for me to speak. At first I assumed that her tears were all about him. But it was a painful cry, not a tender cry, so then I assumed it was all about her freezing feet. Her tiny toes gone numb.

I was wrong on both counts.

Her voice cracked as she spoke.

"I used to be pretty."

There it was. Her simple and profound reality unpacked all at once. Spoken so softly and desperately. Five words falling as gently as a blanket, then exploding upon landing. A riveting memorial to stolen youth and relentless heartbreak.

Frozen tears fell slowly. "Really, I was."

Chapter 9

There she was with her scarred face, poisoned body, dirty rags and big old boots. Seventeen years old, and as far from prom dresses and summer romances as a teenage girl could ever be. I have been among countless young people on the streets, and in the sincerest of all moments—after every ounce of determination and energy has dripped dry—their truest desire is always uncovered. Inevitably, no different from anyone else's: to just be young. Young the way young is meant to be—wishful, dream-filled and full of wonder. Young in a way that knows hope, less bent.

What to say? What not to say? Does it mean anything for a man more than twice her age to tell her she is pretty, in the middle of a very wintry and dark nowhere? And if it does, most likely it conjures up the memory of men who have bartered for or stolen ugly sex with lies, cash and freebees by telling her she is pretty. My place in the moment was complicated and awkward. As I had many times before, I crawled beneath the soulful lyrics in the second verse of Adam Cohen's "Cry Ophelia":

I thank God for my bad memory
I've forgotten some of the stupid things that I've done
I've come to a little wisdom
Through a whole lot of failure
So I watch more carefully what rolls off my tongue.

I had known Tara for many seasons of her long fight to survive. She should have moved on to something, anything, long ago. And still, her trust of me was arm's-length at best. She had told me of others who had crossed her path—some doing their best to help her, and others of more "official" designation who'd simply threatened her with few choices. But she bobbed and weaved between the good-deed-doers and city officials with the same skill and determination that she had done everything needed to get by—including overcoming her addictions.

So I waited on my own reply. I was already deep in the danger zone of one-on-one that every youth worker is warned about. The critical place one arrives at while stretching best-practice policies completely out of shape. Should I follow my heart—and what I felt was God's leading—or play it safe and follow my head?

It is always a gamble to allow impulse to override experience. I know this gamble all too well—and have disappointed and lost many trusts on the street because of it. Finally resigning myself to my routine uncertainty, I played the safe card and betrayed my own heart. And I couldn't help but think hers too. I did not tell her I was sure she was pretty. Or that she still is. And indeed she was, with or without scars.

Dynamite

Under-prepared for simple relief work, and over-zealous for intervention, I did at least have a few bundles of socks in my coat pockets. So, in what must have seemed like most insensitive response imaginable, I tugged a pair out from each of my coat pockets.

"At least they're dry," I offered pathetically.

She cleared the tears from her cheeks and took them. Two pairs. One black, one grey. The baring of a soul spent on two pairs of socks. Just preposterous. Mid-shame, I bounced around the definition of the word *character* in my mind. It bounced back, assuring me that I had been witness to her greatest moment and my worst.

Without hands, Tara shook the boots off. They fell like logs. She quickly peeled her thin socks off and hurried the new ones on.

I could barely look at her, ashamed that I could produce nothing more than men's socks for a girl who needed to know she was lovely, created for love and life, made in God's image and, most of all, pretty. Still pretty.

A few months prior, when the first cold winds began to blow, she had asked me to quit offering to take her to a shelter. I had hinted, suggested and pleaded one too many times. She assured me she knew where they were, and I remember feeling like I was a child being scolded for saying bad words. So this day I did not offer, and she did not ask. But even without words, she knew the offer was sitting fat in the middle of every long pause, and she declined with avoidance.

Tara breathed a long sigh, and thanked me for the socks—in the same way people draw out their words when company has stayed long enough: "Weeeeeell...okaaaaaay then...thank you."

And I traced my drift-covered footsteps back through the snowy bushes towards the pathway, on a long discouraging walk back to the city.

There is a bit of dynamite stuffed beneath every decision one makes. In fact, the word *dynamite* comes from the Greek word *dunamis*, meaning *power*.

Tara lit a fuse the moment she decided to leave her father's house of horror, and the dynamite blew the moment the front door shut behind her. Blast! Tara's very existence had always been about explosive decisions and doing what she could, regardless of all the things she could not. If for no other reason, just to make it to the next day. Smack injections, hooking quickies, hiding in the middle of nowhere—they were survival decisions in the moment-to-moment life of a child taught to expect nothing more and nothing less.

But beyond narcotics and prostitution, there was real dynamite. Piles of it. It took so much more courage for her to hide than it did for her not to. She asked for nothing. She stole away in search of some unimaginable peace and time to sort out who she was, who she could be and what she should do. She was never *"that young hooker crackhead with the scars"* that she had heard others describe her as. No matter who anyone else thought she was, she knew different. The plain truth is that she was one of the brightest lights in the city—one that would not let fire or ice, addiction or perversion extinguish her.

Dynamite exploded around her every single day. Decisions made, fuses lit. Her soul was black with explosive soot, and still somehow it always emerged from the lingering smoke. Not good decisions. Not right decisions. Not acceptable decisions by society's standards. But always brave decisions and hard decisions. Never afraid to set off a charge.

They were character decisions, just like the old man's decision to sacrifice his old toes for her young ones. No questions, no advice, no hesitation or decision by committee. Simply doing what he could. Boots? Okay—BANG! How extraordinary! How fascinating! How New Testament! How absolutely dynamite!

It was while pondering these truths the stormy walk away from Tara that I decided what the next day would look like for me. I made several cell phone calls on the way home, telling friends and acquaintances what was going on. Sad and sorry phone calls that felt like a single stick with a wet fuse. But it was all I had, and God blessed it.

The following morning was beautiful. Crisp, white snow covered everything like cake frosting. I spent the morning meeting up with generous people who wanted to do what they could—a handful of good-hearted supporters buying, giving and praying that their small gestures would mean something special.

Then it was an eager trek back through the snow to find her, two big clean bags in tow. Rounding the final turn, there she was. Busy. Very busy. Tara was folding a frustrating blue tarp. Many of her things were bundled off to the side. I had arrived none too early. Ten minutes later and I would have missed her.

"Enough of this," she said out of the corner of her mouth as she rolled her eyes.

"Where are you going?" I leapt at her.

"Not sure, but I will work it out," she replied evenly.

Then a dramatic pause. She turned to look straight at my face, saying it harshly once again, emphasizing: "*I* will work it out." Leaving lots of space for me to hear the silent "not you."

Dynamite

She gave me a once-over, noticing the bags stretching from my hands, dipping into the new snow. I held them up at shoulder height in front of me. One in each hand. And inside? New winter boots with insulated insoles, a new winter coat with a double-fleece lining, and several more brand new items. Every single one, hand-picked for a teenage girl by people who did not know her. Dynamite decisions and generosity.

For years I have been challenged by skeptics, time and time again, that I am "enabling" the homeless to remain homeless and shelterless by sporadically giving them food and survival items in the midst of building trust. I have been insulted endlessly by people who suggest that I believe homelessness is anything but unacceptable.

But in that moment, far beyond mere survival, far beyond all the awkward untruths and my own defensiveness, there was a beautiful blast! Explosives in the form of gifts for someone who had never known such kindness, anonymous or otherwise. Ultimately detonated by the godspeed opportunity to speak a single sentence, the almost-too-late and right response to a heart broken wide open less than eighteen hours earlier, in the middle of a late-night blizzard:

"These are for you Tara. They will look pretty on you."

Ka-boom! Dynamite. She smiled.

And her smile was so pretty.

June 2005

The last time I saw Ricardo he was rolled up in a ball, teetering on the tip of a cement traffic island–an island in a dangerous intersection, wind-worn by cars running yellow lights and transport trucks not willing to gear down as they approach the highway's on-ramp.

Ricardo had been approaching vehicles, asking for spare change, for several weeks from this unlikely location. Often dizzied by the frenzy, he would routinely find himself stranded between lanes of traffic, looking up at the lights as though they were playing tricks on him. He would wave his gangly arms and shout, "stop it" at green lights, and tell the red ones to "hold on" as honking vehicles whizzed by.

Not in the downtown core, or even near it. But rather twenty-five kilometers northwest of it. Urban sprawl's newest descriptor. A now common testament opposing the media and political myth that if we "outlaw" homelessness in the downtown core, it will go away. Perhaps it will "go," but it will not go away.

Ricardo was a young man with a mind like a child's. His developmental challenges were magnified by the awkward way he moved and his difficulty speaking. His slur made him hard to understand at the best of times, and especially in the midst of a rambunctious crossroads at mid-day. His soiled clothing was always embarrassingly wet. His sleeves were too short, and his pants too high. Brown wisps of hair peeked out from the plaid toque he wore tugged low over his brow.

Everything worked against him. Even the unwritten street code of panning know-how identified Ricardo as highly inappropriate and remarkably unsuccessful. Many times I watched him trip into vehicles as he approached them. Often he would put his face right inside the open windows of cars stopped at a red, drooling on startled passengers and terrifying children. Occasionally, perceptive and gentle motorists would respond kindly. But that was the exception. Repeatedly he would get slapped, punched or have car doors shoved into his ribs. Once I saw a man spit coffee in Ricardo's face.

Ricardo's story was a mystery. He could not recall much of his past, much less tell it. All I knew for certain was that he was forced to leave the small apartment he had received special assistance to get. *"NO PETS ALLOWED."* He described to me the big black letters on the front door sign many times, bewildered that anyone would make such an awful rule. So, he had kept his large and loving dog a secret for many months. With his forefinger over his lips as though to remind me that it was a secret, he would squint his eyes tightly and tell me in his lowest croaking tone, "Naw nevnydody nuvs ma nog, u'know?" (Not everyone loves my dog, y'know?). Then he would shake his head in disbelief. Eventually his secret was found out—some playful barking, a chatty neighbour, and a quick-tempered superintendent all put an end to it.

What was lacking in Ricardo's mind was clearly made up for by the depth of his heart—his wonderfully simple belief that love and affection are priceless, and that shelter is simply a luxury. So Ricardo and his dog survived a long and cold spring along a soggy stretch of the Humber River. Together. Always together.

The last time I saw Ricardo, he was weeping because it had been two days since he had seen his best friend. He was completely heartbroken. His large retriever, Bear, had wandered into the bush behind a nearby brewery and had not found his way back.

The last time I saw Ricardo, he refused to move. Not in and out of traffic. Not back towards the quiet bend in the river below the train trestle where they would often retreat. Just curled up on the paved pad beneath the traffic signals. I offered to look for Bear with him. And if we couldn't find him, we would at least find Ricardo a safe place to be between searches. But he would not accept my offers. He thought that if Bear were to come back, this would be the one place he would know to come to.

If only.

Soft, smart, dirty Bear. A puffy, matted mess of a dog with a tail that never stopped wagging. The only one who Ricardo knew loved him unconditionally. The one who did not laugh at him or fear him. Never hit him. Never spat at him. The one who did not think he spoke funny or looked odd. The one who protected him. The one worth the price of shelter. And most important of all—the one who was willing to accept Ricardo's love. Big old Bear. Simply gone.

I have met countless young people and adults on the streets, ranging between unaware-of-the-world and absolute genius, who are no different. Owners of street pets, beautiful and strange. Hundreds of dogs, cats and kittens of all shapes and sizes. Pet store rats and gutter rats. Lizards and snakes. Mice as pets, and mice as dinner for those lizards and snakes. Ferrets, pigeons, baby raccoons, turtles, a Black-Handed Spider Monkey, a Norfolk Grey Chicken and something that to this day I still believe was an armadillo. You name it, I've seen it. And as traditional or odd as the pets and pet owners have been, one thing is always the same: every owner longs to find some way to love and be loved, without being hurt. The very thing we all long for.

Ricardo stayed at those lights for days. The police shuffled him off from time to time, but he just waited in the wings until they left, and then hobbled back to his place amid the stop-and-go motorcars. No more asking for change or startling strangers. Just sitting, waiting, crying and praying out loud: "Thear Thethuth, brin mi ba ma Ber." (Dear Jesus, bring me back my Bear.)

Without the burden of pride or self-consciousness, Ricardo emptied his weary soul in plain sight of the busy world. Mother Teresa once said, "Love, to be real, must cost, it must hurt, it must empty us of self." To apply her beautiful words to a man and his dog may seem blasphemous at first pass. But not for this man, this dog, and this love. Real. Cost. Hurt. Empty. It was all there.

Six or seven days later, when I went to bring him a bagel and hot chocolate, he was not there. Perhaps, I thought, at the donut shop restroom, or back behind the brewery getting something from his hidden belongings? So I crossed into traffic and left the bag and cup at his spot. I returned the next day, and it was sitting there untouched. Even the birds and traffic winds had left it alone.

For weeks I stopped at those lights every day, longing to see Ricardo stumble haphazardly into traffic, with a big brown Bear only a few feet behind, tied to a piece of clothesline. I prayed at those lights with all of my being. I prayed for small miracles unknown to me. I prayed that a man and dog had found each other and that they were pouncing around like a boy and his puppy. I prayed for gentle strangers to come along and become protective and safe friends. And I prayed most of all that God would make my own heart as pure and tender as Ricardo's. That I would know always to make priorities of the heart the highest of all my aspirations.

There is a verse in the Old Testament that I think of when I remember Ricardo. "The Lord does not look at the things man does. Man looks at the outward appearance, but the Lord looks at the heart." (1 Samuel 16:7) A verse that should make 99 per cent of Western civilization tremble, and a verse that makes someone like Ricardo anything but a developmentally challenged, homeless man. More than anything he is an ambassador of God's own heart—the highest of all callings.

The first time I saw Ricardo, the day we met, I asked him what I thought was a simple question: "Why are you trying to collect change at this busy, dangerous intersection?"

His simple answer was profound and spectacular, pointing east with a crumpled hand, speaking slowly to be sure I would understand.

"Ith nee du ped sor, an thumtime we ged hunry." (It's near the pet store, and sometimes we get hungry.)

Indeed, I had watched him share a can of dog food with Bear more than once. And with nothing but thanksgiving for the food and the one he shared it with.

Oh to be loved like Bear. Oh to have Ricardo's heart.

When President Mikhail Gorbachev launched a policy of *glasnost* in the Soviet Union in the mid 1980s, the last thing on his mind was how a new style of music called "grunge" was changing the North American pop music landscape. When the wheels of *perestroika* were set in motion to bring about economic reform, tropical fire breathers were not part of the equation. But, shortly after the Revolutions of 1989 that overthrew Soviet-style communism, rock and rollers of all shapes and sizes and hula dancers in grass skirts were on their way to Eastern Europe. For better or worse.

Along with folk singers, concerto musicians, puppeteers, mimes and poets from around the world. In the midst of all of these was the hard rock band I was in at the time, Double Edge, traveling to St. Petersburg, Russia, for a concert on New Year's Eve in 1991.

Chapter 11

Just a few months prior, this was the last place in the world I would have imagined myself preparing to sing "Auld Lang Syne." The whirlwind schedule that brought us there included cultural-awareness classes, crash courses in Soviet politics, hurried travel preparations and bizarre fundraising measures. We ended up on a global bill for the "Sacred Fire International Christian Arts Festival," pulled together by a charismatic troop of artistic visionaries under the banner of Youth With A Mission.

It's hard to know what we accomplished. I must admit that, as we set out, the outcome for the people of St. Petersburg, Russia, was not as big a concern for me as it should have been. When an unsigned band is asked if they want to gig overseas, the first response is always yes. Less than 10 per cent of most young band experiences include playing in front of a paying audience. And that's if you're lucky. The mathematics for unsigned bands playing predominantly original material is not at all good—particularly for a band with a faith-based message. It takes thousands of hours of other things to pull off hundreds of hours of performances. Writing, practice, lugging equipment, equipment malfunctions and problem sound checks, driving-driving-driving, lost, stuck at the side of the road, self-promotion and time spent speculating how the next gig is "the big one"...just to name the top ten.

So, when someone says any of the following words: overseas, roadies, hotel, production company or all meals provided—you don't even stop to think.

The journey to Russia was akin to the band adventures we knew only too well. A friend from another band on the bill awoke mid-flight to find his leg completely frozen to the inside wall of our tiny rattling airplane. We literally had to pry him off. I had to change seats because the back of mine was not attached to the bottom. Some of the seat belts had no clasps so we were instructed to just tie the ends together. We waited in a Bulgarian airport for hours while organizers tried to figure out why there were no planes, and why our group was not on any itinerary. During a fueling stopover in London, England, they actually opened the "only open in an emergency" safety doors to let in fresh air. It was clear: we were not touring with the Rolling Stones.

Still, once we arrived, none of it mattered. We were in Russia! The military statues were bold with sharp lines; men with fierce gazes and jutting jaws. The roadways were wide and tank-parade ready. The wind was cold and unforgiving, shaking the bus as it blasted against the side of it. All of it looked and felt just like the Russia we thought we knew from the movies.

Late at night, as the bus pulled to a creaking stop at our hotel, blurred silhouettes of adults and children appeared through the frosted windows. We stepped out slowly, one by one, as though we had landed on Mars, into a crowd of aliens. "Please, please. Trade, trade. Buy, buy. Good, very good." The simplest of English words straight to the point. No one wanted a handout. They had too much pride for that. Bartering was the business of survival here. They desperately wanted to make trades for Russian nesting dolls by the dozen, wrinkled paper replicas of famous paintings from the Hermitage Museum of Art, and all sorts of military paraphernalia and garb, including valor and service medals, fur *ushanka* hats, entire foot soldier and officer uniforms. It was all up for grabs.

Among the group of ambitious trade merchants were several children, some with their parents and some alone. One little girl stood at the end of the line. She couldn't have been more than eight years old. Her long scarf was draped over the top of her head and wrapped around her face, so that all we could see were her wee red eyes. Tired and cold. Though she could barely be heard, from beneath her scarf I could see her little mouth moving as she held out two little babushka dolls, "Please, buy."

Once in the hotel lobby, we all paused in bewilderment. This was not about "rock-and-roll." This was about real, unforgiving, relentless life. The looks on the faces of the other performers was not unfamiliar. It was the wide-eyed look of shock and disbelief. The teary-eyed look of helplessness and embarrassment. The anguished look of knowing we have grotesquely taken our blessings for granted, and today is the emotional and spiritual day of reckoning.

Our travels through St. Petersburg were astounding. The majesty of the great city was a sharp contrast to the desperation on the streets, brought on by the frenzied and unthinkable political and social changes. At one point we walked past a line of people for two city blocks. They were lined up for a store that was rumoured to be getting cheese. Straits so dire that rumours alone were worth lining up for, for hours upon hours. Minute by minute our own purposes for this St. Petersburg visit seemed less and less significant.

While our nighttime gigs met our expectations—with huge P.A. systems, enormous lighting rigs, exciting venues (including one great hall that once held communist headquarter events), and a teenage audience eager for the sounds of North American hard rock and heavy metal—our daytime bookings were something completely different.

Our very first concert was an afternoon event in a small theatre. We went early for a sound check, then waited in the back for our cue. The theatre was clearly a performing arts auditorium, and our off-stage green room was a dance studio, complete with stretching rails and wall-to-wall mirrors. As we sat in the back, we could hear the faint buzz of people filing in, and we were eager to get out there and make some music on foreign soil.

Just before the concert, we snuck to the side of the stage to get a peek at the audience. Sure enough, it was a full house. But, to our amazement and horror, the room was filled with children—some as young as four or five years old, and none older than eleven or twelve. But not all were the same. Some were children of culture and social privilege, attending with their classrooms and educational chaperones. Little girls in frilly dresses with big bows, and boys in crisp white shirts, red and gold vests and shiny black shoes.

And then there were the others. Orphans. The "lucky" ones sponsored for the day to do something they had never done before: a day trip. Hair combed straight back, yellowed shirts awkwardly tucked in and pressed as best as could be expected for the strange outing.

Of all the tragedies to haunt the souls of the Russian people, none is as compelling as the overwhelming issue of orphans. Hundreds of thousands of children exist in underfunded, understaffed and over-populated state institutions. With inadequate nutrition and insufficient emotional care, many of these beautiful children are, and will remain, underdeveloped both physically and mentally. Some authorities estimate that as few as 5 per cent of the children in Russian orphanages fit the technical definition of orphan—which is "a child living with no parents." The truth is that most of Russia's orphans do have at least one living parent, and many have both. The lion's share of state orphans are children who have been abandoned or rejected by their parents, or whose parents have had their parental rights denied for irresponsible behaviour, born out of issues such as addiction, neglect, criminal activity, and/or the vast perils of extreme poverty. These young ones are known as "social orphans."

We scurried back to collect our thoughts, mind-boggled. We had spent years crafting hard-hitting songs about street justice and social alienation. We had forged an intense sound that grew heavier and heavier to grip hardcore Western teenagers enthralled with sex, drugs and rock-and-roll. We had nothing to offer the tiny children of St. Petersburg.

Our saving grace was the newest band member, Bevan. While the rest of us had been together for many years, he joined just prior to our Russian journey. Bevan had moved across the country to marry our guitarist's sister, who is also my wife's best friend, and was invited to join the band when he arrived. (Bevan's story goes on to be one of the most devastating that my circle of lifelong friends has ever endured. Just months after our return from Russia, he was struck by lightning and died on the third day of his honeymoon.) Bevan's musical roots were not as deeply submerged in the hard rock genre, and he had a gift for creating softer sounds. In a frenzy, the band reworked simple classics into child-friendly rockabilly nuggets, while I met with an interpreter to sort out simple Russian lyrics that I could sing phonetically. The children smiled, laughed, applauded and sang. When it was all over, we stood side by side, waved, bowed and ran off the stage like children's performers in big dinosaur and teddy bear costumes. And while it was the most awkward gig I have ever played, it was also perhaps the most memorable.

When it was over, I wandered out to get some fresh air, clear my head, and be alone.

I made my way through a series of unlit hallways towards the rear of the building and came to a seldom-used metal door. I pressed the panic bar to open it, but it barely budged. The snow was piled against the outside of the door, and the more I pushed, the more the snowy barrier resisted. Finally, I just threw my shoulder into it until it opened just enough for me to squeeze through sideways.

Outside the door was a storybook courtyard. About twenty-five metres in diameter with several alleyways converging between the backs of the old buildings, it was a quiet, snowy hideaway.

And right in the middle were two small children—a boy about seven, and a girl about five. Lying on their backs making snow angels, they were caught off guard to see someone emerging from the door that no one ever used.

I waved and smiled. The boy lay perfectly still, looking worried and scared. But his sister lifted her mitten and waved back—a sweet little wave as if to say "we know we aren't supposed to be here, I hope we are not in trouble, but hello anyway."

I stepped through the drifts on the stairs towards them. The boy stood as he saw me coming, then motioned for his sister to do likewise. She popped up and giggled. He turned to reprimand her and she stood silent. They both wore ragged, poorly fitting coats. She had bright blue mittens on, and he wore mismatched men's gloves. Both wore oversized boots with dragging laces. Ragamuffins to a tee.

"Hello. What are you doing?" I asked.

They looked up at me and said nothing. So, I asked again, foolishly, thinking that saying it slower would somehow help.

They both began to speak hesitantly in Russian.

We didn't understand one another, but we all tried our very best. I pointed to their snow angels and gave two thumbs up. The little girl ran over to her imprint and drew a halo above it. And for a few surreal minutes, I got lost in the

Chapter 11

tiny world of their make-believe space, where the only toy was imagination. Just me and two tiny children in a hidden Russian courtyard, trying to understand one another and enjoy this moment of community. A gentle reminder that the world is so big, and yet so small.

I knew I needed to depart soon from their magic little world, so I began my sad goodbyes. I reached in my coat pocket and pulled out a package of brightly coloured gumballs, each no wider than a penny. One each in red, blue, green, yellow and orange. Some of the many treats we were encouraged to bring to share with the children we met.

I held the package out to the children. Their eyes widened and their jaws dropped. The boy took off his glove and slowly raised his open hand. He wouldn't dare reach for them in case he misunderstood, so he just placed his little open hand in front of his chest wishfully. I placed them in his hand and stepped back.

"*Spaceba. Spaceba,*" they said, thanking me in hushed voices.

I nodded and thanked them as well, for welcoming me into their sacred space—a place where poverty and wealth were not pitted against each other, and a place where forgetting one's poverty or hunger was easy because dreaming was allowed.

I stepped back into my own deep footprints, in and out of the banks of snow drifts. Just before I went to wedge myself back inside, between the door and the casing, I turned back to say goodbye one last time. But I did not. They were lost in yet another world. One much better than watching a stranger close a door on them and return to his absurd blessings.

There they were, kneeling at either end of a block of wood. The little boy took out one small gumball, then carefully wrapped the package up and secured it deep in his pocket. With the tiny ball between his thumb and fore-finger, he began to carve it with a piece of scrap metal. He worked with the focus of a surgeon, while his sister watched, barely a nose-length from the whole operation.

He held them up to the sky, to see that the two halves were even. The little girl could barely contain herself. She was bouncing on her knees begging him for her piece. Finally, he placed it in her mitten.

But they did not consume them. Rather, each took the time to study their own tiny halves. To appreciate the most miniscule of treats. To ponder the joy of having something special.

They were like cherubs in the snow. An absolute vision of innocence and purity. A picture of what the electricity of thanksgiving should be. And as far from the self-indulgent notions of rock-and-roll as anything could possibly be.

Finally they agreed it was time. They counted together, then placed the gum in their mouths. While they giggled with delight, I snuck back inside and closed the door as gently as I could, so the sound of my departure would not be heard.

We went on to perform at least once a day for the remainder of our time there. Most days we played twice. Big gigs, small gigs, dry ice and stacked amp gigs, and more children's playhouses. As mixed a mixed bag as is imaginable for any band or performer. But the gifting in it all had nothing to do with the music. Nor was it ours to give. Quite the contrary, it was ours to receive. We visited several orphanages and were reduced to puddles in the process. As a peculiar angle on our band and small entourage, all of us happened to know sign language and had been significantly involved in southern Ontario's deaf community. Thus we had special invitations to visit orphanages that housed deaf children. The small fingers of deaf orphans signing so descriptively is perhaps the most exquisite sight I have ever seen. The wear on our hearts was both merciless and priceless.

A few months later I was serving an afternoon shift at Frontlines Youth Centre, back in Toronto. After extracting the final belligerent few testing me on closing time, I locked up the front and side doors and made my way to the back of the building. I opened the big metal door that exits into the fenced back lot. There, beneath an arching basketball stand, were two small children playing in the melting snow. A boy and a girl. Underdressed, wearing loose-fitting sneakers, and soaked through and through. There were no adults in sight. My heart all but stopped as I saw them. Surrounded by government-assisted housing and inside a community with economic and social stresses, this was not a new sight for me. But they were so overwhelmingly reminiscent of the young ones I had known so briefly on the other side of the world.

I wore a coat that day that I hadn't put on in months. Not since the Russian adventure. I reached inside my pocket for my truck keys and pulled out something I had all but forgotten: a package of brightly coloured gumballs. Remnants of my Russian stash.

Kids should never take candy from strangers. And guys like me should know better than to test them. But I lost my sense in the moment.

Sure enough, my gesture was accepted. But I didn't want to stop and watch what might happen. I feared they might just gulp them all at once, thanklessly and without appreciation, in keeping with so much of North American culture. So I darted to my truck, and pulled away.

Chapter 11

But curiosity got the best of me. Just before I reached the bend in the lot, I stopped and looked back.

I saw two small children on their knees—the little boy carving a gumball in half with a key, while the little girl consulted nearby.

Children nations apart, with little more than age, snowfall and scarcity in common, somehow demonstrating the richest virtues of godly character without effort, and unknowingly sharing their great wealth with me.

Oscar Wilde's quote penetrates my heart as I think of children such as these: "Ordinary riches can be stolen: real riches cannot. In your soul are infinitely precious things that cannot be taken from you."

Author's note: The events of this chapter, and the statements made about gun reporting, occurred several years before gang-related gun incidents began to escalate rapidly in Toronto. I am quite sure dialogues with officials and my own response regarding personal liability would now be very different.

"You know what this is? You know what this is in your face? A Beretta! A Beretta!"

Beretta compact and subcompact handguns were principally designed for personal defense. Serious firearm enthusiasts carry on about their reliability and durability—but the street knows them best because they are easy to conceal.

Over the years I have seen several guns peeking out from beneath untucked shirts and bulging from the cuffs of pant legs. Nothing sits so heavy in the pit of my stomach as the terrifying sight of a gun in the possession of a teenager.

Completely unnecessary for most homeless young people, the young hardcore street dwellers who do choose to pack semi-automatics share the same claim as the countless knife toters—defense. However, in the mind-bending world of addiction, the line between defense and offense is illegible. Early on in my years of street outreach, and often, I approached police and policy people at every level, investigating the complexities of what I should do, need to do, and should want to do with the unsettling knowledge of handguns and their possessors—trapped by the reality that there is no greater requirement for meaningful and sustainable street work than street credibility. Credibility teetering on non-negotiables that include not ratting or squealing. Of course, the jolting flipside being my own liability, responsibility and guilt.

Chapter 12

The sight of a gun on the streets is always unnerving. But on this day, for the moments it literally bridged the lives at either end of it, this gun's presence was spellbinding. That the white-knuckled hand that held it could have changed so many lives so instantly was simply overwhelming. Its black profile was just 18 inches from my face, lodged between a young stranger's hand and the forehead of the trembling boy beside me.

I had just sat down beside a very stoned and withdrawn Jerrad. He was 17 years old but had a measure of sorrow that better suits someone who has lived a full and tortured 77 years. We were perched on a cement divider that hedges the south end of the city's biggest sports complex—home of the Toronto Blue Jays. Jerrad was slowly rocking back and forth, in and out of the thin vertical shadows of the wrought iron guardrails in the mid-day sun. The sad and easy movements of an addictive high disguising themselves as escape. Moments of false escape that steal lives. Few words. Several long sighs. Just the glazed moments of his drug-induced high before the ultimate crash that would follow. The unspectacular reality of street life that regularly consumes time like a giant plodding monster.

Then instantly, as though someone had shoved him headfirst into a pool of ice water, he came to. Staring straight ahead, leaning into the shade, and cursing in quick unfinished phrases, he was suddenly alert.

I turned sharply to see what had caused this incredible bit of voodoo. The silhouette of a lean figure with an unruly mop of hair moved in rapidly. The stranger stopped directly in front of Jerrad, and without a moment's hesitation pulled out a charcoal-coloured pistol, and held it directly between Jerrad's eyes.

"You know what this is? You know what this is in your face? A Beretta! A Beretta!"

Seconds felt like hours as their anxious dialogue told the ugly story. Jerrad had broken a sacred rule on the street, and had stolen from one of his own. A friend. A brother. Family. Sure...street friend, street brother, and street family...but in the unreal-and-too-real social structure of street culture, these are bonds with their own unique values and consequences.

The devil's recipe on this day: cocaine hydrochloride mixed old school with baking soda. An addiction too powerful, and a temptation too great. A few rocks of freshly cooked crack that might as well have been nuggets of pure gold. Every element heightened by the unspoken and sordid details of how one gets and pays for drugs and guns in the first place. Not always with money. So there we were...gathered in one place by the unquestionable code of the street: *payback!*

Threats and excuses were wildly exchanged. The stranger's finger never left the trigger and the gun tip never left Jerrad's brow. Within minutes Jerrad was holding out a dirty little bag with a trembling hand, stuttering pleas in his thick French-Canadian accent.

The young stranger was livid. He dug the gun tip deep enough into Jerrad's head that it began to bruise and swell.

"That's half. Where the rest? I will kill you! Right here and right now!"

And me? Shoulder to shoulder with Jerrad. Inches from the barrel. Neither person involved acknowledged my presence as they negotiated betrayal and justice.

If he pulls the trigger, should I run or try to jump him? If I run, which direction? Pathetically, these were my responses to playing any kind of significant role in the outcome. I'd like to call what I was doing praying, but it wasn't. I just stared at that gun. Stuck in the moment, staring.

It was a single and slight movement that finally woke me like a slap across the face. The stranger angled his wrist inward as he pressed forward, mimicking feature-film images of street criminals ready to take the next step. Jerrad muttered, "Dear God," and mumbled half-stoned, half-panicked prayers to live. English, French. French, English. Startled, I looked at him and recognized that even in his half-baked state, he was in a zone that I, shamefully, had not yet reached: asking the life-giver to preserve life.

With at least a hint of my wits about me, I spoke my only words in the entire episode: "I'll give you whatever is in my wallet for this to be over."

And they both looked over at me as though I had popped onto the scene like a genie. They had forgotten I was even there. The shaggy stranger glared at me and jolted his head back as if to say—well, what do you have? I reached in my pocket and took out three crisp twenty-dollar bills I had withdrawn from a bank machine that morning. For several seconds we all held our places in silence while he thought it over.

Finally, the stranger snatched the small bag from Jerrad's jerky hand and plucked the bills from mine. He pressed the pistol one last time into Jerrad's pink forehead, gave it an angry shove and turned away. Looking back, he reminded Jerrad that he was "lucky." He stopped for a moment to bury his Beretta, stash and cash in his loose clothing, and departed.

If I spent a lifetime doing absolutely nothing but describing Jerrad, "lucky" would be the last word I used. An alcoholic by age 12, as a small child he was his mother's door guard while she dealt drugs from their Montreal apartment. He never knew his father and, apart from a few minutes one night, neither did his mother.

Chapter 12

On this day, hope—even bent hope—was a blur at best. It is so difficult to find anything redeeming, but for the thorny notion that God hears even the prayers of a lost, stoned, panicked boy, barely keeping his head above water.

I never saw Jerrad again. Some kids beneath the Bathurst Bridge told me he returned to the streets of Montreal the very same day, fearing for his life.

I was simply there, caught in the Russian roulette of timing. No gun at my head. No payback due. No addiction. No ridiculous history of fending for myself since childhood. Not homeless. Not unloved or unwanted. I went back to the safety and peace of my home, family, friends and all the things missing from Jerrad's life. And a teenage boy—who should simply have been worrying about things like grade 11 mathematics and football tryouts—was running for his life.

Surely Jerrad's crimes are pale in comparison to the crimes committed against him throughout his entire young life. Ambiguous crimes that are collectively ours to own. Tribal crimes of neglect that allow a boy to arrive at young adulthood staring cross-eyed into the shaft of a pistol, begging to live. Philosophical crimes as simple as misinterpreting what it means to live out the old adage: "We take care of our own." Ethical crimes that have us spending more time pointing fingers and debating over fault than looking for answers. Or, worse still, simply choosing not to be part of the answer at all.

But perhaps the worst crime of all is that so many followers of Jesus have not been able to interpret a magnificent passage from the New Testament with an extra measure of creativity and grace that would make it relevant in the lives of so many just like Jerrad. The words of Jesus in Matthew 25, verses 35 and 36:

For when I was hungry—*you understood that the sustenance of food is just a start, and that I ache for the nutrition of education, work, play and a sense of home*—you gave me something to eat.

For when I was thirsty—*thirsting for joy and the opportunity to feel good about who I am and who God made me*—you gave me something to drink.

I was a stranger—*a stranger to innocence, tenderness and mercy*—you invited me in.

I needed clothes—*to be clothed in safety and peace and rest*—and you clothed me.

I was sick—*sick of running and living in desperation, sick of never belonging or fitting in*—and you looked after me.

I was in prison—*the horrific prison of addiction and all the terrors that brought me to that place*—and you came to visit me.

Verse 40 of that chapter says, "I tell you the truth, whatever you did for one of the least of these...you did for me."

Gun

When stories of street weapons and drugs come up, the discussion that follows is always about justice. We make no mistake in tying these issues tightly together and insisting on creating order and securing our own safety. Surely the first descriptor of justice in the New Lexicon Webster's Dictionary sounds familiar to all, and gives voice to what we desire most: "Behaviour to one's self or to another, which is strictly in accord with currently accepted law, or as decreed by legal authority."

This is the justice of courts and law enforcement.

But for the Jerrads of the world, justice, more than anything, needs to be found through the filter of Matthew 25. Buried beneath the vibrato of the dictionary's first descriptor is a second that resonates with this seldom-realized truth about what justice can be, should be: "Rectitude of the soul enlivened by grace."

Justice as a gift, not as a punishment. Justice as life-giving, not as a consequence. Justice "enlivened by grace," not born of fear. And most of all, justice for the Jerrads, long before they are forced to run for their lives.

Justice that has nothing to do with judges or juries. The kind of justice that opens hearts wide enough to know for sure that this story is not really about a gun at all.

April 2000

Tall. Tanned. Well-dressed. He marched towards me double-time, grinning from ear to ear. He shook his head up and down as though he had won a bet, and then back and forth as if to say, "I can't believe it."

"I knew it! I knew you would be here! I knew it!"

He giggled it over and over as he approached me.

A stranger? Yes, surely a stranger. I could not place his deep voice, his healthy face or his eager step. Sitting on the curb at the southern tip of Spadina Avenue, I could only guess that he had confused me with someone else. Likely someone homeless.

Very often, because of the places I frequent, the way I appear and the people I am among, I am mistaken for a homeless man. Over the years I have been bear-hugged by tearful strangers sure that they had found a long-lost family member, and spat on by outraged strangers who were certain they had come across an old enemy. Once a man shoved me around and cursed me for ten minutes, positive he had stumbled across a university buddy who had stolen his girlfriend years before, yelling, "You see what you get? What comes around goes around! Look at you now! A nothing! I would love her to see you now!"—before I could convince him I was not who he thought I was.

At least this stranger seemed friendly as he approached. Very friendly.

"Well...hi," I shrugged as I backed off the curb onto the sidewalk.

Chapter 13

I stood in front of him with a blank smile, ready to work through this mistaken identity, just as I had done so many times before. His eyes were as wide and bright as silver dollars, and his smile filled with the kind of pride a child gets rushing home with a good report card. But as thrilled as he was to see me, it was clear that what he really wanted was for me to see him. He stepped back two paces so I could get a better look. Every few seconds he spread his arms like a magician when he ends a trick with a big "taa-daa!" And I just kept on disappointing with a big dopey smile.

He began to laugh—a good thick belly laugh. He was delighted that I didn't know him.

"Aaah, man!" he snickered.

With a silly grin across my face, I sighed apologetically. He snorted and rubbed his hands together, as though he was ready to get to work. He popped the dome on the left sleeve of his jacket, his deep laugh dulling into a soft chuckle. With his left hand clenched in a tight fist, he used his right to drag the sleeve of his bomber jacket all the way up to his elbow. No laughter, no chuckles. My eyes welled up. I looked up at him and his eyes filled with tears. But the smile never left his face.

Tyson.

It was Tyson. I was completely awe-struck. I gave him the once-over he had been counting on. Then again, in disbelief, head to toe. He looked fit and proud. He had broad shoulders, white teeth and healthy skin. I stepped back to take it all in at once. It was incredible. He was incredible.

Then my eyes returned to his extended forearm. The carvings had dulled and smoothed over the years, but the wide scars were still shockingly familiar. They represented the passage of time. They were the markings of a painful youth that he had survived, and of my best efforts—too little, too late. Or at least I had thought so at the time. And they were the powerful reminders of years that had vanished without me noticing. Four white and slightly raised letters.

FEAR—dug deep with a switchblade during a stoned rage. The dreadful calling card of panic. He was only fifteen at the time. Six years earlier, only a block away from where we were standing, I helped clean and dress these same self-inflicted wounds. I remember that the E in particular bled so badly through all the gauze and wrappings, that I begged him to let me take him to the hospital. He had lost so much blood that he was almost passing out. But he would not go. Just snap to every few seconds and grab something to wrap over the last wrap: a dirty sock, an old shirt, anything he could scrounge from his pack.

That One Acorn

When I first met Tyson, he was picking up cigarette butts along King Street's famous theatre district. The area was famous for half-smoked cigarettes because people would jump from their limos and taxis, light up out of habit, only to realize they needed to butt out and rush inside before curtain call. All in all, for the average street warrior, it was a great stretch to score free nicotine.

That day, Tyson was sporting two black eyes, the whites streaked with blood—fading keepsakes compliments of a chronically abusive dad far, far away. Tyson hit the ground running when it came to street life. Within weeks he had bottomed out in every destructive way possible. He knew it. He was purposeful in it. He used needles the way hungry babies use bottles—grab, devour, toss. A decade and a half old, fast-tracking the learning curve on what it means to "live to die." By the end of his first month on the street, I anticipated his death daily, and so did he.

Then about two weeks after his cutting, he turned. It was the very day he undid all the bandages. We were lunching at a hot dog cart outside the west entrance of Union Station when he dropped his shoulders and sighed, "This is not me." It was as though his soul had been absent for a season, away on an unannounced vacation, and had decided to return home—just swung the door open and cruised inside declaring, "I'm back!" He was bright and alert and confident. It was beautiful. It was the answer to the ceaseless prayer I ache for, but that I am often too desensitized and weathered to anticipate.

"I need out. I'll die here." He ran the back of his right hand over the dry scabs on his left arm. "I need out."

We spent the better part of that afternoon mapping out history on the back of a napkin, connecting the dots on a sketchy family tree that spread from Halifax to Victoria—from an uncle to a second cousin to an ancient grandmother. We needed a safe place far from throwaway smokes and street vendors' leftovers. Eager for immediate escape, Tyson entered Union Station that same day, headed west and vanished into the next unknown that, no matter how it turned out, had to be "better than this."

There is a pain I have come to know guessing, wishing and hoping for the best. Early on, I was naïve about what it meant for someone to leave the street. I was eager to believe that being off the street was the finishing line of one race, and the starting line of the next. But of course, it is really just a watering station during a marathon—a significant one for sure, but still very far from the line. Tyson's miraculous and sudden inspiration and the train ticket west were simply the first watering station along the way. A history of abuse, neglect and addiction were all still chasing him, anxious to trip him up.

Chapter 13

But even in the largest of marathons, filled with thousands of runners, eventually someone wins. Someone crosses the line, throws up their hands in magnificent disbelief, and feels it is a miracle.

Yay Tyson! I thought, and wished I had been at the finish line to witness the glory.

Tyson the man had twenty minutes for me. Twelve hundred seconds on the stopwatch. In a rushed trip to Toronto, he squeezed in the search for me at the tail end, just before a mad rush back to the airport. Back home.

He laid it all out at fever pitch, desperate to fit it all in. Grandma had the heart of the Prodigal Son's dad. There was a man at Grandma's church near the coast who helped teenagers get into special school programs. He was hooked up with all kinds of ace contacts: an addiction counselor, a distress therapist, and a co-op work placement. And Grandma made sure the meals were warm and the clothes were clean.

Tyson went on without stopping for air. And now? A third-year university student in a southwestern state. Engaged to another student. Attending a local church and volunteering with a food bank. He spoke without breaking stride and I listened in shock. His mouth never stopped moving and mine hung open, still. Twenty minutes to tell the miracle of a lifetime. Every second filled with his joy and my fascination.

He looked at his watch and stopped, mid-sentence, hesitant for the first time. He began shuffling sideways, "I gotta, well, I gotta ...ah...I knew it! I knew I'd find you!"

I became dizzy just watching him twist in circles, calling back to me as he headed north up Spadina. I was eager to race up the street with him, flag a cab with him, and sprint through the airport begging for more details. But I had changed lots too in those six years. I knew what it meant for someone to leave the street, for them to make it to the next watering station. Almost always, it meant not going back. His quick hunt, his healthy stature and his beautiful rushed story were a gift to me. But they were not the cues of a return, or some messed-up nostalgia. The last-minute timing alone was an unspoken message from a boy barely into manhood struggling to look back over his shoulder briefly while still running the race. So I made no chase and gave no phone numbers or promises.

Finding health–real physical, emotional and spiritual health–is a prospect that, more often than not, seems so unlikely. And miracles seem like fairy tales when you are cutting into your own flesh.

Who knows what form a miracle will take, or when it may occur? I didn't bother trying to predict God's miracle of a new Tyson, because I didn't even have the faith to expect it. So many of us pray for miracles every day and go about expecting them never. But they happen every day regardless of our ignorance. Stars, worlds and worlds away, poke holes in black skies every single night. We sigh and look away. Birth is miraculous and new every single time it happens. We sigh and look away. And mighty oaks grow from acorns that survive ridiculous odds: squirrels and blue jays hiding them away, beetles nesting in them, even wet leaves covering them until they rot and mould. We don't even sigh, we just look away. Still the mighty oak tree is known best for its endurance and strength. Some giant oaks can live for hundreds of years—undaunted by storms, disasters and the unpredictable forces of nature. But only one out of every ten thousand acorns that fall to the ground survives to become a tree. Miraculous. One.

I stood silent, waving conservatively to that one acorn as Tyson faded north. Distance can be a rich and fertile soil.

I heard shuffling footsteps behind me. There stood 15-year-old Michael—ripped clothes, smeared face, torn sleeping bag draped over his shoulder and a squeegee in his belt loop.

"Who's that?" he asked, looking back and forth between me and the great oak jumping into a taxicab.

"That's you. I pray to God, that's you." I answered.

He shook his head, grunted and walked away. Towards the squirrels, blue jays, beetles and wet leaves.

Where do they go? When do they go? Why do they go? What happened?

All those limbs. All those digits. Disease, war, torture, abuse, accidents, one-in-a-million freak incidents. The street owns volumes of these stories.

When people walk by, I always wonder why they don't wonder. Maybe they do.

There are so many people surviving the streets of North America missing arms, legs, fingers and toes that it is almost shocking. While most children are authentic enough to stare wide-eyed, point and look terrified, the extreme opposite response from most adults is almost comical.

Of all the voyeuristic moments my time on the streets has allowed, none is so consistently mesmerizing—almost sadistically entertaining—as watching people pass by a dramatically physically disabled person panhandling or selling pencils, flags or buttons. Most people simply pretend they do not see the person, while taking in what they can from the corner of their eye. The giant white elephant crowding the sidewalk, so to speak. It is standard operating procedure for most people when it comes to the homeless, limbs or no limbs. Then there are a few who will drop a few coins in a tin cup or ball cap and make believe they do not notice the absence of entire body parts—as though arms and legs are no big deal. A fraudulent kind of nonchalant "oh well, some of us have 'em, some of us don't" approach. For others it is more of a "maybe if I don't say anything, they'll think I didn't notice" type of thing. Even more absurd, "maybe he (or she) will just not think about it." While, no doubt, there is an awkward best effort somewhere in there, for the most part, it is also a testament to a world that has not figured out how to be authentic and kind at the same time.

Chapter 14

I have never met a man or woman on the streets who was not appreciative for the acknowledgement of their affliction. Not by merit of pity. But that such a loss, and living with such a loss, is part of their story. Empathy found between gawking and pretending.

Oddly enough, it has often been along boardwalks and docking stations on both coasts that I have seen or met many amputees living on the streets. Some have told me sea stories about their lives that sounded more like living-in-the-belly-of-Moby-Dick tales than reality. But the tears in their eyes as they gazed over the watery horizon always made a believer out of me in the end.

I once sat on the pier of a maritime harbour and watched an episode I will never forget. A wind-worn old man in a skipper's hat, with a wiry beard, was propped up in his rickety wheelchair. He had no arms or legs. Well, technically, he was missing one arm completely, another from the elbow down, and both legs gone below his thighs. Pressed between stumps that ended with knees was a coffee cup, and resting against his misshapen belly was a sign that simply read "God Bless You"—an image almost too profound for words, even before noting the obvious.

I believe that when any person who is homeless asks for God to bless anyone else, it is on par with angels deciding to clean our toilets. Anyone who is not humbled by the mere sentiment has already lost a ridiculously large portion of their soul. The small hand-scribbled signs alone, scraped on cardboard, are sacred documents. Words etched on paper tablets by hands that have endured hell on earth to write them. But the words said aloud, from the curb skyward, beneath rumbles of traffic and snorts of exhaust—these are the ignored voices of heaven. Of all our shames, this perhaps is our generation's greatest: that we long for high priests and clergy royalty to bestow these words on us, and disregard the tender gift of receiving them from where the cost is truly immeasurable.

And when the one who offers it up has no arms or legs... it borders on insane. I am quite sure that I would want my sign to read: "Are you blind or have you lost your mind? Look at me! I am homeless. I am sitting here all alone. I have no arms. I have no legs. How much more has to happen to me before you give a damn?" Of course, I would need someone to write it for me.

On this day, there were the painfully obvious questions. Like how did he get there? No one else was nearby. He was literally all alone. Did someone roll him there, set the cup and sign in place, and make plans to pick him up later? If so, did they get a commission? Who dressed him? Fed him? Put the hat on his head?

I sat and wondered—could a human being be any more vulnerable than this? Physically? Emotionally? Spiritually? What is the internal cost of being rolled out to pan for change? Left alone in the sun and wind among tourists and seagulls? If it was me, what if I had to go to the washroom? What if I had to blow my nose? What if my entire existence had finally worn me to nothing and I simply wanted to blow my own brains out? Life, death and everything in between—all things, as I could only ignorantly imagine it, at the request of favours.

As I sat and pondered the incomprehensible, the Atlantic winds blew. Salty gusts would rattle his wheelchair, and he would negotiate them by wiggling his torso into the back padding of his rolling chair, all the while keeping the cup from tipping between his stumps. But the wind was relentless and, sure enough, he began to tip like a tree with weak roots in a sudden storm; slowly, and in tortured inches. He arched his neck back and tried to throw his weight in opposition to the wind, but physics and gravity fought him. Still, even as his body involuntarily bowed, there was no look of concern on his face. No signs of worry for what looked imminent. His courage was remarkable.

People continued to walk by, the pretending all the more fierce as his body leaned at forty-five degrees. I stood to my feet. I had planted myself a fair distance from him, but not so far that I might not still beat the next blast of wind if I bolted.

Sure enough, just as I leaped from my perch, that next mighty blast rolled in. It was more than powerful enough not just to knock him down, but to lift him several yards high, have him hover several more and then roll him in a frenzy along the pier.

But in that same moment, a sentinel appeared. Bounding from behind a cement breaker wall was his unassuming guardian angel—a magnificent, plump First Nations man with a long salt-and-pepper ponytail. With the strides of a deer he blew in from nowhere. In bare feet, with his open shirt spilling his belly over his beltline, he raced across the boardwalk. His wide hands fell on his friend's shoulders at the very moment he began to levitate. The old man in the chair didn't even blink. He knew the forces of nature had nothing on his best buddy.

With his left arm wrapped tightly around the old man, the hero dropped to one knee at the side of the wheelchair. What happened next symbolized all that hope—even bent hope—can be. There were great shouts of laughter. Though I could not hear their conversation, the laughter between sentences was glorious. The chuckling while trying to get the words out was splendid. The man with all of his limbs used his right arm to gesture all that could have happened, all that looked inevitable. Wind, elevation, and bouncing angles—he painted the picture in the sky with his right hand, never releasing his left from around his friend's shoulder. The old man with no limbs smiled wide and nodded, chiming in with his own colour commentary. And they laughed and laughed and laughed.

How does a man who exists without the most basic of human blessings find joy in escaping one more perilous moment? He simply finds joy in knowing who he can trust, and then actually goes about trusting him. Radical trust that takes radical courage—the kind once spoken of by Mark Twain: "It is curious that physical courage should be so common in the world, and moral courage so rare."

In this case, the old man takes that courageous conviction and reciprocates by never questioning that trust, and then giving back whatever he can: thanksgiving, joy, kinship, delight. The best of what he has to offer; making the most out of every shared moment.

They are imperative life lessons, survival lessons, hope lessons and God lessons about what trust looks like for people with limbs or without. In homes or without homes. Rich or poor. Male or female. This is the glorious result of unquestionable trust. Earned, given and most of all, shared. Radical in its simplicity. Extraordinary when executed without effort. And exquisite, just as I had witnessed it.

April 2007

While hope may well be the music of the soul, peace is surely one of the sweetest instruments playing the lead. And, if so, there is no finer commissioning than the Prayer of Saint Francis, which begins: "Lord, make me an instrument of your peace."

One of the grandest metaphors literally connecting a musical instrument to the notion of peace is a national icon that rings with glorious song, gracing the skyline of Canada's capital city, Ottawa. The Peace Tower stands 92.2 metres tall, directly in front of and joined to the Centre Block of the Canadian parliament buildings, where 308 members of parliament (including the prime minister) convene to make decisions on behalf of all Canadians. Originally built to commemorate the end of World War I, the Peace Tower also contains one of the most renowned bell instruments in the world.

The Peace Tower carillon is a 60-ton instrument containing 53 bells of various weights and sizes. The carillon is played from a massive keyboard, requiring fists and feet to press the huge keys. The music that rings from the Peace Tower is magnificent.

How profound that it was there, with the noonday sun rising over the waving Canadian flag mounted atop the Peace Tower, I would meet a man so broken, so tender and so longing for peace.

Just a few days earlier, my friend Julia and I had met a man with no legs and

Chapter 15

only pads for hands in Ottawa's Byward Market area. A sweet old man panhandling more for the purpose of meeting people than gathering loose change. We had stopped to talk with him, and before I noticed he was missing more than just legs, I reached out to shake his hand. He lifted his right arm and placed his fingerless pad inside the palm of mine, and smiled. Then he placed his left pad against the back of my hand and squeezed as best he could. His eyes reddened as though no one had tried to shake his hand in years—or at least since he had fingers. He squeezed my hand at length as a reminder to me, and perhaps to himself, that he was no less a gentleman now than ever, regardless of all appearances.

His imprint was fresh on my mind when, a few days later, I met yet another man with just a thumb on one hand and a half thumb and two half fingers on the other hand, just a kilometre west, in the long shadow of the Peace Tower, directly below its bells. He was in an ancient wheelchair with big wheels at the front and small at the back. It could have belonged in a medical museum or been hidden away in a forgotten war triage bunker. One of his legs went as far as the kneecap. The other went all the way down to his ankle, which rested inside the opening of an old business shoe.

He was staring up at the flag and humming. I smiled and stepped closer to his side. When he peered up at me, he smiled a great tight-lipped grin, his bottom lip touching the bottom of his nose. Clearly, no dentures. I was just about to ask him what he was humming when I recognized it. In a creaky low hum he was buzzing the national anthem.

While the Royal Canadian Mounted Police colour guard in full regalia and fireworks shooting above the parliament buildings are the epitome of national pomp and circumstance, somehow this weary old man humming from his antique wheelchair was the most spectacular and heart-wrenching moment of Canadiana I had ever experienced.

At the three-quarters mark of the anthem he broke from humming and began to sing, "God keep our land, glorious and free...," and then returned to humming the last small portion. Then he looked back at me and smiled again—a great toothless smile that wrapped its way around his face.

"Thank you," I said, smiling ear-to-ear myself. "Thank you."

"Son," he said, nodding his head sideways that I would draw near. I bent beside him to listen. "This world has taken lots from me...." He held one padded hand in front of his face and slapped his leg with the other. "It has not been kind to me, took all my loved ones, took all my dreams...."

His voice began to quiver as he gestured for my hand. He took it between his withered paws and placed it against his chest.

And Still Another: The Dealmaker

"But son, no one can take my heart. It's a deal I struck with God."

Then he lifted my hand from his chest, kissed the back of it and held it against his cheek.

And without a shadow of a doubt, in that moment I was positive that I was somehow holding the very hand of God. It felt neither misshapen nor damaged. I held it firmly with honour and love, as though it were precious. Through all the pains of his ancient life, this man knew the tenderness of the Almighty. Past the horrors of a life twisted by hurt, sorrow and the sins and frailties of humankind, he still had a voice to sing. And with the sad hope of finding sustaining peace at the foot of the Peace Tower, he poured his soul out before me and gathered me up that I too might touch a bit of heaven.

I will never know what deal he thought he struck with God. Deals with God are most often considered the talk of heretics. But I don't care about that. I believe that if a deal did go down, it was because, while the world worked against him at every turn, God knew and treasured his heart.

And he, like so many others living on the streets who scrape and scramble through life without body parts, can be perfect in eternity. Already, as far as I can tell, he is more perfect on earth than most of those who pass him by.

He kissed the back of my hand again and held it against his cheek. Then he sat high in his wheelchair and spoke boldly, as though revealing a secret hookup with God, more divine than I or anyone could know.

"Son, you go now. There's lots to do."

Blessed and sent, I went in peace.

Prayer of Saint Francis
Lord, make me an instrument of Thy peace;
where there is hatred, let me sow love;
where there is injury, pardon;
where there is doubt, faith;
where there is despair, hope;
where there is darkness, light;
and where there is sadness, joy.
O Divine Master,
grant that I may not so much seek to be consoled as to console;
to be understood, as to understand;
to be loved as to love;

Chapter 15

for it is in giving that we receive,
it is in pardoning that we are pardoned,
and it is in dying [to ourselves] that we are born to eternal life.

November 1993

"Like an unchecked cancer, hate corrodes the personality and eats away its vital unity. Hate destroys a man's sense of values and his objectivity. It causes him to describe the beautiful as ugly, and the ugly as beautiful, and to confuse the true with the false and the false with the true."

Martin Luther King Jr.

Hate is death. Nothing more and nothing less. Even if the heart pumps blood through the system, a life of hatred is a dead life. When the anger and fear of bigotry are woven in tight knots that spiral around the core of one's being, the essence of life is strangled. The tighter the weave, the tighter its squeeze on life.

Richard's street name was "Hit,"—a street tag short for Hitler. I have always tried to honour street names by using them if young people really wanted me to, but only if they were not belittling or devaluing. So I refused to call him by his. I always called him Richard. He said he didn't like that, but I didn't care. I also didn't believe him. By age 16, Richard was bound by hatred like a mummy. Wrapped in it from head to toe. Wound with layers upon layers of hatred, cocooned in violence and intolerance. Dead long before he was dead.

At the time, I was the director of a youth centre called Frontlines: a joint venture between Youth Unlimited and my home church in the city's rugged northwest end. We had just moved the project, after a three-year stint in a tiny storefront rental space, to a new building courageously purchased by the church I have attended my entire life—Weston Park Baptist. A key element in the vision for the Frontlines outreach was peacemaking. For several seasons in a row, the corner of Weston and Lawrence had become media popular around issues of racial violence, backdoor drug running and low-track prostitution. It was heartbreaking for long-time Weston dwellers, many of whom had been part of this historic community for generations. But the church, with 85 years of sacrificial and inspirational commitment already under its belt, believed that the glass was half full, where so many others had given up on it as half empty. And they invested in an abandoned tavern, less than a block south of their own sanctuary.

I was so excited about the new building that I would go in early every day and stay into the wee hours, just to help rip up rum-drenched carpets and plug holes in smelly grease traps with rags. There were countless jobs to do once the deal was done and the building was ours. The giant walk-in freezer was full of food, but the electrical power had been shut off several months previous. A co-worker, Andrew, and I spent an entire day, each wrapped in plastic hooded suits, wearing surgical gloves and masks, running in and out of the freezer whipping toxic vegetables and furry meat into a bin while dodging huge cock-roaches and angry rats. But it never felt like anything but an adventure. A won-derful adventure: to stake a claim in the shadowy corner of my own childhood community, where I truly believed that ugly insects and rodents would be exter-minated as quickly as the notion of violence and injustice. There I was, still young enough to believe it, and just old enough to survive my own naiveté.

One day I was returning from the local hardware store with supplies for the day's chores when there was a commotion beneath the overhang at the front doors. Two teenaged boys all in black leaned against the building's long front windowsills. Even from a distance they were easy to identify with their eggshell scalps and knee-high boots. They were picking pieces of garbage out of a trashcan and throwing them at people walking along the sidewalk. Taunting almost everyone. But especially and assuredly—anyone not white.

"Stop it! Stop it!" I shouted as I darted across the street.

Just as I hit the curb, they nailed a young Somali boy in the head with an open plastic bottle, half full of orange pop. He looked terrified as the bright soda dripped down the right side of his face. He started to run. They plucked out tin cans and half-eaten bag lunches, moved to the centre of the sidewalk and took aim, laughing and mocking him with every pitch.

"No! No! No!" I insisted.

They cursed me out, spat at my feet and moved back to the windowsill.

"No. You don't understand. Not here. Not ever," I preached.

"And who the hell are you?" one sniffed at me.

"I am the one who can insist you get off the property." I held up the door key, much to their surprise.

Something about a young disheveled white guy in charge piqued their interest, and their tone changed. We spoke for a few minutes, and I invited them in. They looked around the open space, bewildered.

"This place is what? You're gonna do what here? You're nuts! Wasting your time." It wasn't the first time I had heard any of it. Just the first time I had heard it from a pair of skinheads.

Their heads were round and pale, with just a hint of fuzz like worn tennis balls after a season of ball hockey. Both boys had glossy white swastikas framed in red piping painted on the sleeves of their leathers. Richard was lean. He had a long scar over his right eye—apparently from a north-end neighbourhood cleansing attempt. His friend, Dog, was thick and wide, with no neck. A big round head plunked onto a torso like a snowman.

They were only 16, but Richard in particular was indoctrinated in the movement more religiously than most evangelicals are in theirs. Before they would listen to my views, they put me through a screening process. I responded to one probe with a comment about British and United Empire Loyalist roots on both sides of my family, and they nodded with arrogant approval. They interpreted this information as a sign that it doesn't get much whiter than me.

Dog was a giant. He looked fierce. But his eyes revealed something different. He was lost in the mayhem of it all, like a trapped animal, confused and spinning in circles. Richard, on the other hand, looked as though he could be snapped like a twig. But what his body lacked in physical prowess and intimidation was made up for by the relentless scowl on his face and contempt in every word. He was sold on the horrific purpose of it all.

Dog seemed like the kind of big lug that would nervously patrol a jungle in wartime carrying a massive machine gun, praying he would never have to use it. Richard seemed like the type that could grab that gun out of Dog's hands and start shooting madly at anything for any reason. A woman cleaning her hut. Children playing with stones. A big bird in a tree. No rhyme, no reason.

The neo-Nazi movement in Toronto was significant through the 1990s. It was driven by an underground hate-music scene—one that the city became known for among white supremacists all across North America. I occasionally went with Richard and Dog downtown, to surreptitious events and ad hoc gatherings. There I met dozens upon dozens of Hits and Dogs seeking identity and a quick place to belong, entering mindlessly into an evil pit of brainwashing. Kids selling their consciences to the synergy of a militant room and the colour of their skin. Promises of kinship. Starving for truth and choking on lies.

Over time I was accepted by them as a bit of a "loser adult," with nothing better to do than hang out with these young people. In their view, I was a possible convert. I sensed their expectation that if I fell in with them, at the very least I might have some money and resources for the basic necessities, if not for the cause. I found that many of the young people buying into the scene were actually homeless—young people who would not use the shelter system, drop-ins or meal programs in the downtown core. Many of them faded fast. Not real believers. Just searchers, taking a foolish and sometimes deadly pit stop on a bad-to-start-with journey.

Dog left the ranks only two short weeks after I met him. "Just another traitor who will learn what's what," Richard assured me. A week after he left the scene he began hooking up with a Latin girl on the streets. One night at a Cherry Beach shanty, they were beaten within an inch of their lives. They both vanished the following day.

But Richard—he represented that rabid faction that breathed the ideology. He got high on it and never came down. A white disciple, clinging to the cliff-edge of racism by his fingertips. Twisting in the wind of imminent death while laughing ferociously the entire time. He was terrifying!

I kept up with Richard for several months. I would finish my day at Frontlines, get a burger to go, and take my pickup to the city core to spend time with him and the bewildered cast of characters hanging out with him, that came and left without conviction. Richard began to lose his mind in it all. He truly went crazy. If I took him to a corner pizza shop to buy him a slice, he would not take the food, no matter how hungry he was, if a white person had not prepared it. He began mumbling to himself about his cockeyed views and hate-mongering, oblivious to the world. Soon enough, he was babbling about himself in the third party, a victim of his own sick and tainted mind.

"Everyone's missing it. Everyone's lost. Hit, only Hit gets it. Hit knows. White is right. Hit knows."

Many scary, life-threatening and ugly months later, Richard and I found ourselves sitting at the base of the City Hall's arching observation ramp. He spoke with calmness—the first I had heard from him in seasons.

"You. You're the only adult I've ever trusted." Those are rare words that awkwardly affirm a street or youth worker's calling, and pay their emotional dues.

I thought maybe I should have been thankful. Surely this was a compliment? But no. Something in the moment deeply disturbed me. His voice was sharp, and his grin was toxic. I started to feel sick and responsible. Here was a boy who sacrificed his entire existence looking for a place to belong and only felt accepted when attached to hatred. A boy slithering into manhood, still choking on lies. A life I pitied and despised simultaneously. So I just sat quietly, trying to convince myself that this was his offering to me.

But I failed. Instead of allowing the moment to ease down on me, I grew angry. Angry at Richard. Angry at Richard as Hit. Angry at his mom not present and his father never revealed. Angry at a cowardly and hidden regime. Angry at God. And, when I finally finished pointing my finger at everyone in my brain, I reached me. Me, with all my own biases and bigotries that I had convinced myself were okay because they were little and quiet, unlike the overwhelming possession of Richard's disease. Me, who had a boy trusting me because I fed his hatred with compassion and failed attempts at reason. Me, angry with me, because I came face-to-face with my belief that Richard did not see the two of us as much different from each other.

He looked at me and grinned. He could smell the fear in my anger, and the anger in my fear. It was a scent he knew better than anyone. His voice was smooth and evil.

"There is only happiness in hate, Tim. Hate is the cleanser, Tim. We fix it. Then, then there is joy." He spoke like a demon.

He stood and stretched. Then walked away, like a cat with a belly full of mice. Satisfied and sorrowless.

All alone, later that same night, he placed a pistol in his mouth and went looking for whiter pastures in heaven, hell, or whatever he thought might be on the other side. He pulled the trigger. He swallowed a bullet, but the lies are what he choked on—Adolph Hitler's own hideously ironic words: *"Our strategy is to destroy the enemy from within, to conquer him through himself."*

The night he died I went home to hold my baby daughter. I snuck into her little room and gently reached into her crib. Softly, I lifted her into my arms. She was only five months old. She was tiny. She was perfect. And so innocent. So unbearably innocent. I pleaded with God to spare her. To send his chief angels to keep watch over her and lift her above every dark creature and every dark world. From everything and anything that looked and sounded like Richard. I begged God.

As I prayed, tears fell on her sweet face and startled her. She flinched and gurgled. And in the midst of her cooing, God spoke to me. Not words and phrases. No writing on the wall. God has never spoken to me that way. God spoke to me the way only God does, with his gentle hand resting on the shoulder of my soul. And in the bundled movements of my sinless baby girl, he reminded me that Richard was once just like this.

Tiny. Perfect. Innocent.

His.

Never be afraid to trust the unknown future to a known God.

     – Corrie ten Boom;

       holocaust survivor, humble hero and author

December 1998

Time alone with a group of street kids is always sacred. Always. To experience the kind of trust that allows one to be welcomed into their secret presence is a gift impossible to describe. There are precious moments when frailty and brokenness are revealed, completely unguarded: an authenticity like I've found nowhere else, and with no one else. Moments when full disclosure of the heart and soul are more brilliant and more costly than gold, frankincense and myrrh.

And among hurting people, young and old, even the hardest hearts soften some while resting in the lap of the Christmas season. On every frosted street corner that knows a homeless life, an undefined sadness and beauty lingers. And on one particular night, the magic of what Christmas is meant to be was not lost on the brittle and sentimental hearts of my young friends.

Five of us were huddled beneath the lowest incline of the Spadina on-ramp—a quiet hideaway for stolen youth, fleeting dreams and broken hearts.

Chapter 17

One of the city's many dark resting places for teenagers dodging their way through addictions, abuse and neglect. Even so, late on a blustery Sunday night, the steady hum of busy lives racing around in warm automobiles seemed more pronounced than usual—a weighty reminder that the rest of the world had somewhere to be.

Earlier that evening, the west-end church I attend hosted their annual carol-sing. A traditional church basement evening filled with the hallmarks of a small church family just being a small church family. Good people gladly taking in the sounds of a noticeably out-of-tune upright piano, the relentless feedback of a small 30-year-old P.A. system, and the smell of coffee made in an urn that never leaves any church basement. After the cozy family-friendly event, several foam plates overflowing with homemade leftovers were assembled with care, covered with silver foil, and sent away with me, along with the truest of best wishes.

When I arrived under one of the nation's busiest urban exits, four grey faces turned my way. These teenagers were living as castaways, staring into the tide of complete homelessness and all that it really means, watching their note in a bottle sink.

As I drew closer, I called out "Homemade treats!"

Each syllable delivered its own tender intimacy: home, made, treats.

Home—the word least spoken, and most longed for. The dream of what it could and should mean.

Made—created for enjoyment. Intentional. Detailed. Prepared with care.

Treats—something extra, something special. Something beyond survival. Something with a nod to feeling like a child again.

All put together, at that time, in that place, they were the happiest and saddest words ever to have met.

The sight, the smell, the touch and, of course, the taste stirred all the senses among a very eager group of recipients. Nostalgic recall rolled into tragic emotion, opening deep wounds that had never been dressed or even begun to heal.

"My mom used to make these," young Sarah said softy, holding a sparkling cookie in her black mitten. She held it as though it were priceless and meant to be guarded, not consumed. "It is the only thing I can think of that I miss," she continued.

Sarah, 17 years old. Hard. Hard the way people paint portraits of old sailors on weather-beaten sea vessels. Tiny slits for eyes staring into wild storms with determination. Hard in the bravest and most stoic of ways—ways that say, under every circumstance—no matter how bad it looks ahead, it's better than what's behind.

Sarah was for the most part a loner on the street. She represented that eerie part of the sailor's portrait you don't know for sure, but just assume. That is, that the sailor is manning the boat all alone. It was uncommon for her to hang with the three others that were gathered that evening. In fact, it was uncommon for her to hang with anyone.

Her comment about the cookies became a springboard for an intriguing conversation about homespun Christmas traditions—a conversation that unrolled into one about the original Christmas. Then about what it might have been like to be present at the very first Christmas. There were donkey jokes and cattle imitations, and small doses of quick-witted humour that keep minds sharp in the saddest of times. I have known few mortal beings who can pierce into truth like young people, adults and seniors who are homeless. Brilliant, sublime and painful all at once. But in this moment, just enough of an attempt to breeze away any relapse into the serious and thoughtful comments that hurt so much. And it worked for a short while.

But in the end, at this season, to deny the heart inevitably became too much work. As the lulls between jokes and wisecracks grew, it was 16-year-old Dougie, from the farming fields of southern Alberta, who braved his way forward. Incredibly bright and kind, Dougie had a special gift: he would not let the hardness of the street betray his heart. Quite the opposite approach to Sarah's, he often hedged his bets for emotional survival on opening his heart as wide as possible. Every young one is so different, unique, so very delicate, no matter how hard they might appear.

While folding a sheet of pressed tin foil from one of the plates, Dougie commented that, "the baby Jesus probably got tired of everyone hugging him."

Then it came. Quietly, gently and from out of nowhere. As though unaware that she was actually speaking aloud, Sarah surrendered, "I've never been hugged."

And we all sat in silence. But for the slow chewing of shortbread, and the quick whistling of frozen rubber tires racing above our heads, it was a surreal, heartbreaking silence.

Henri Nouwen's cascading truths, written in his book *Out Of Solitude*, ring true in moments like these, both on and off of the streets. He said:

"When we honestly ask ourselves which person in our lives means the most to us, we often find that it is those who, instead of giving advice, solutions, or cures, have chosen rather to share our pain and touch our wounds with a warm and tender hand. The friend who can be silent with us in a moment of despair or confusion, who can stay with us in an hour of grief and bereavement, who can tolerate not knowing, not curing, not healing and face with us the reality of our powerlessness, that is a friend who cares."

Eventually, curiosity stole the last mouthful of a star cookie, and 18-year-old Chantal leaned in, "Never? Not by anyone?"

Sarah responded twice, back to back, with the same words.

"No! Never!" Very angry.

Then again. "No. Never." Softly, sadly.

My mind began to wander, swept up in the unthinkable tragedy of a young life so betrayed by the notion of love. I kept thinking about my two children. My baby boy, Jake. My own sweet daughter, also named Sarah, some 12 years younger, hugged and kissed with the same natural instincts that cause me to breathe. Every day. Over and over, every single day.

Then, in an instant, I returned to the young survivors as they stood up one by one. Up from the splintered freight skids and frozen buckets. Compelled to rise by no other prodding or instinct than their God-given hearts. Then and there, teenagers tagged daily as misfits, delinquents, beggars and losers responded like angels sent directly from heaven, commissioned solely for Sarah. Each one stepped towards Sarah and, one at a time, without saying a single word, took her into their arms. And she melted there. A tiny Christmas miracle in the hidden winter shadows of absolute compassion. No twinkling lights, no presents, no music. Just some leftover baked goods, four priceless children, and a man who witnessed Christmas angels revealing themselves eight feet below the rusty steel girders of an ancient motorway.

A night like no other.

A silent night.

A holy night.

June 1994

"Doogan, come out. It's okay, it's just me."

He stood silent, then dropped inside the bin. "No. Just, just...no. Go away."

"C'mon bud, you're gonna get sick." I stepped up against the rusted wall and spoke just loud enough for him to hear.

There was a long pause. Complete silence, but for the sound of gluttonous flies hovering everywhere.

Finally came the awkward sound of a human gaining balance on two metres of loose garbage. His grey fingertips reached over the lip of the dumpster. His feet bounced and slid against the metal sides. Then his body flopped over onto the ground. He reeked. His sweating body had absorbed the stench from inside the bin like a sponge.

There is no more self-defacing act in street life than dumpster diving, and no more ungodly dichotomy than the fact that people less than ten metres away are eating like royalty.

He looked up at me reluctantly. Smeared across his face was—well, it was hard to know what it was. It appeared to be a horrid mix of yellow mustard and mayonnaise and the green leafy ends of some sort of rotted vegetable. The sick look on my face told him in an instant, and he proceeded to wipe his chin and cheeks with the tail of his shirt.

"Don't say anything. Just don't, okay," he said sheepishly as he smeared his hands along the ground. Then he lifted his foot repeatedly and stomped his toe back on the ground where his heel had been. A strange act I had seen him do often.

It was all strange. The boy was too proud to pan for change, but not too proud to dumpster dive for dinner. Several times he had told me, "My dad says the only thing worse than a murderer is a beggar." And every time he told me, all I could think of was the Japanese proverb that says: "It's a beggar's pride that he's not a thief."

Of all the backwards words of misguided wisdom gleaned from his father, few would turn out to be more costly than these. But even in the wickedness of his newfound poverty, he carried oozing vats filled with the ridiculous standards of his father.

Doogan's dad had beaten him for failing to get the grades he needed for entrance to the university of his father's choice. Certainly not the first beating, but surely the worst. It was a maple dining room chair smashed into his face and his father's own devilish challenge that pressed him out onto the streets.

When I first met him, four days into the street, his face was caked with dry blood. Over and over he repeated his father's decree: "Come back when you make something of yourself."

Doogan grew up within the luxury and curse of great wealth. Never wanting for anything, but always searching for something. Like all those who arrive on the streets, from rich homes, poor homes and everything in between, he was homeless long before he was houseless.

While a house can be described by appearance and physical details—red bricks, black roof, four bedrooms, hardwood floors—what a "home" is meant to be requires soulful consideration: a place of peace, joy and belonging.

One portion of The Ottawa Manifesto (created and released by StreetLevel: The National Roundtable on Poverty and Homelessness in 2006) clarifies the difference.

It reads: "A home is more than just four walls and a roof. It is a whole life situation that means being welcomed into a safe, secure and dignified place to live; healthy, nurturing relationships; the opportunity for education, meaningful work for meaningful pay; and to worship, dream and play in vibrant community."

Doogan grew up inside beautifully decorated walls and rooftops designed by master architects. Mannered and refined in a mansion. But when he fled, it was surely not from a home.

He always kept me guessing. He would do anything he had to do to get what he needed when people weren't looking, but would never allow his appearance to betray him. Thus, he never begged or panhandled. He would steal like a bandit to avoid being dressed in rags. And he would curse like a banshee when we were alone, but never a foul word in public. The keeping-up-appearances bone his parents had rammed down his throat was lodged there for good. He remained faithful to the code, and simply adapted to the circumstances.

"Let me buy you something to eat. You've got to eat," I offered.

"I did eat. Fools throw out the best parts of their meals." He refused me, as he had so many times before. "But I do gotta clean up."

So we hiked to a nearby mall, and I waited at the foot of the escalator. When he emerged a while later, he looked like he was on his way to ask a girl from prep school to the senior prom. His hair was slicked back. His fresh duds were crisp and clean. He was tucked and trimmed to order. Quite remarkable some 30 minutes from the bin. I didn't even bother to ask how he did it. A stash kept in a mall locker? A slick move in a change room? A barter for some "other" currency from a teenage shopper or street acquaintance? It was Doogan, so it was a whatever-it-takes proposition, and as he played it out, no one needed to know any better.

As we walked out of the mall, we passed by a young man panning for change. He sat timidly with his legs crossed so he wouldn't block the walkway. His old cap was set in front of his knees. And he simply said "hello" to anyone who made eye contact.

Doogan looked at him then back at me. He rolled his eyes and muttered, "Pathetic."

A parent's legacy to a child is a mystifying and powerful force. Even as Doogan was forced now to live out the life of a schizophrenic rat, he was still trapped by instants of seeing the entire world through his father's eyes.

"Pathetic. What a nuisance."

The irony of his words against his own actions was sublime, and the calamity of his perception tragic. For in those moments, he became his own cruel father. A flat-screen outline of a human who perceives life and death as a single dimension and bases it all on convenience and appearance.

Many people view homelessness that simply. From the outside looking in, it is a one-dimensional issue—a nuisance. Half-breathing lumps on heating grates, grimy faces on unhygienic bodies, unsightly belongings left abandoned in doorways and people too stupid or lazy to get on with their lives. It's ugly. It's horrible. The whole mess is a repulsive nuisance. From water coolers to talk-radio, this is the best-known dirty face of homelessness.

And if "nuisance" is the marker for identifying the target issue in most people's minds, then panhandling is the red flag showing shooters where to aim first. The catastrophe of homelessness, the foreboding root causes, the spiral of lives broken and dreams lost, all shortchanged by the inconvenience of passersby having to say yes or no. Of having to look to the side and acknowledge a living being, or stare straight ahead and play make believe.

Chapter 18

While this book is anything but tangent-free, I have nonetheless done my best throughout to run the asides where they best belong and in context to the story at hand. Based on the level of debate this particular issue receives on a constant basis, and its great relevance to Doogan and his story, I find myself overwhelmingly compelled to include here a complete commentary parallel to this story.

There is no discussion that I have been asked to comment on more often than that of panhandling. Forceful by-laws, punitive resolve and hard-line decrees regarding the issue are now part of the fabric of urban dialogue. If ever I have heard generally pleasant people sound cruel it is over this matter. If ever I have heard reasonable people say ridiculous things it is over the same.

And while "aggressive" panhandling is the verbiage used to lower the boom, from street level one thing is abundantly clear: aggressive response to panhandling is by far the greater and more common crime. While I have witnessed over the years very few verbal tirades from panhandler to passerby, and not a single physical altercation from sidewalk to pedestrian, I have not only witnessed but also been the recipient of—as people have assumed me to be homeless while sitting next to my street friends—endless verbal and physical assaults directed the other way.

My experience tells me this: if you call someone a beggar then I already know where you stand. Too far into the illusion that I may be a bleeding heart on this issue—still, I believe I am not. I am a father who frequents the downtown core with his children more often than most. I am the friend of many people who work in business towers and run stores on main streets where people panhandle in the greatest numbers. I am one who appreciates the esthetics of cleanliness and understands the important economics of tourism. One who considers good stewardship both a moral and spiritual issue. And I am one who would like nothing more than to see the streets free from panhandling.

But free of it because people don't need to do it. Not because we have made extreme poverty a crime. Sadly, I confess I am like so may others who feel the same way: not sure of what the solution is, but very sure of what it isn't.

And while cities all across North America debate circles around the issue with surprisingly little creativity, individuals still want to know what they should do. It is quite simple. If you don't want to give someone your money, then don't. If you do, then do.

However, be assured that the act of engagement and the opportunity for esteeming someone through an unrehearsed kindness of any kind can quite often change the way the day unfolds for people at both ends of the exchange.

A Canadian one-dollar coin is worth one hundred cents. No matter who owns it, no matter what is has been spent on in the past or will be spent on in the future. In one's hand, as a tangible object, it is worth one hundred cents for all of time.

However, the act of giving that coin away can be priceless. Not when it is tossed begrudgingly into a hat or coffee cup. It remains a one-hundred-cent prospect. But when someone takes even a moment to bend from the position of power, to make eye contact, to wish someone well, and then to give away something of value without any condition or presumption, the worth cannot be measured.

Do some people use their money for drugs and alcohol? Yes, some do. But not in the frolicking way fraternity brothers buy kegs. It is more often in the same manner any grieving addict succumbs to an illness that steals the best in life and offers the worst.

I find the book of Proverbs in the Bible is like a playground for the scripturally challenged. Something compelling for everyone, including those with meagre attention spans and limited awareness. A place where you can jump around quickly and move from the wisdom slide to the truth-telling swing and back to the what-on-earth-does-that-mean monkey bars all in a matter of moments. However the impact is best when appreciated slowly. It is a volume filled with bite-sized treats that last like gobstoppers. You could take just one and work on it all day long.

In the final chapter of a book whose purpose is to promote wisdom and godly living, two verses come as a surprise. Amid an oracle taught to a king by his mother, it says: "Give beer to those who are perishing, wine to those who are in anguish; let them drink and forget their poverty and remember...no more." (Proverbs 31: 6,7)

As these verses stand alone, what they seem to lack in judgement, they more than make up for in being non-judgemental and understanding. Of course, a broader and full gaze over the entire passage reveals the verses in full context. But even still, just in and of themselves, there is something sweet in the immediate sentiment of the verses. Not in condoning, but in consoling.

While all of these issues are truly overwhelming and complex, the answer to the next question is certainly just as important. Do *all* of them use their panhandling money for drugs and alcohol?

Chapter 18

Absolutely not. Food. Socks. Underwear. Saving for a bus ticket to get somewhere else. Birthday cards to send to siblings in group homes and family members in prison. Cold medicine. Foot powder. Nail clippers. You name it. I have known people to panhandle for a first month's rent so they could get off the streets for good.

Then there are the discussions of fairness and value-based responses. People who worry about the fact that people panhandling do not pay tax on it as an income. Or those—and yes, they exist—who will give a five-dollar bill and ask for change or reach into a coffee cup to get it. And of course, those odious enough to threaten sarcastically to do it themselves: "I should just go and do that. I would love to sit around all day and just get money for doing nothing." Oblivious to the cost of humility and humiliation.

Here is my advice to all those who say they want to give to people on the streets but are worried they will just spend it on drugs and alcohol. To the many who have brought this discussion to me, lost between the little cartoon devil on their left shoulder and the angel on their right. Spend not a moment longer worrying or fussing about it. Warm regrets and simple smiles should abound, for whether you give or do not, whether you seek the mind of God or believe there is no Almighty, this is a human encounter. And if indeed it has been a complex emotional bother to you, set aside a jar on your kitchen windowsill, or at the corner of your desk, and every time you have gently said "no" to a person panhandling, take the coin you decided not to give and put it in that jar. And when the jar is filled donate it to a mission or outreach or program that you know will use the money well for those who are homeless. Be released from the strife caused by the battling little voices in your head telling you it is a bad idea. But do something that will at least dam the flooding hypocrisy of speaking this great concern and doing nothing.

And indeed there are many thoughtful people approaching it from a different angle who often come out of their encounters feeling disheartened and frustrated. I cannot tell you how many times I have responded to these comments:

"But I offered to buy someone lunch and they refused me!"

"But I offered them part of my lunch and they refused it!"

"But we got a group together and came down to pass out bag lunches and some people refused them or didn't appreciate them!"

To exasperated concerns such as these, here are some of the many things I have found myself saying:

"While we spend an abundance of time discussing how scary homeless people are to everyone else, have you ever thought you may be scary to them?"

"I hate bananas now, they make me gag, and even if I were homeless I would still hate bananas."

"If one person appreciated it, and it was meaningful for them, would that be enough? How about two? Three? Okay, four? How many would make it worth it?"

Enter in with your good heart, and keep it intact. That you have tasted discouragement and rejection when doing your best is not a surprise. I have spent my life simply praying that God would bless my best intentions, regardless of how I thought things should be.

I know how people *on* the street and *from* the street and *of* the street use the money they pan and beg for. I have seen them gather it, spend it, lose it and waste it. And still, often I give a buck or two to those whose smiles and faces touch me, and the occasional bill to those whose voices resonate with my soul. And always, I am thankful that I have. You should always be smart and thoughtful with your resources and time. These are blessings, not rights. Then set your conscience to this question: How many ways do I abuse, misuse and take for granted the blessings in my life that hold no reasonable comparison to the risk of what may happen when I compassionately give a few coins to someone on the streets? Whether you give to someone panhandling or not, the answer to the question is yours to own. Just as it is mine.

And back to Doogan, for whom begging, in any shape or form was simply deplorable.

After we had passed the young man panning in front of the mall, Doogan turned and faced me, while looking at him over my shoulder, then down at his feet, and back up again. Once again he lifted his foot and tapped his toe against the place his heel had been. The very strange habit he fell into whenever there were still moments.

He pulled his hands out of his pockets to help him make one last grand statement about the importance of appearances. Out of his pocket fell four large felt-tip markers. He dropped in an instant, retrieved them and shoved them back in his pocket, while I looked at him sideways.

"Ya, found them somewhere. They were new, just thought I would keep them."

While he playacted through the story, the foot tapping became quicker. Toe back to where the heel had been.

Chapter 18

But the truth was clear, even without admission. Sniffing and huffing highs are cheap and quick. Volatile solvents such as felt-tip markers are common entry points into the brain-twisting world of inhalant abuse. Aerosol sprays, gases and nitrates all wait in the balance as part of a menu that often starts with cheap fixes such as sniffing glue or breathing in household products. Or in young Doogan's case, simple magic markers.

I tried to hang in there with Doogan over the weeks that followed, but his descent into the city's most rapid addiction was fast and furious. Soon I became familiar with the parking lots he liked to frequent. Large lots near the lake where pedestrian traffic was minimal, and where one could easily hide while killing countless brain cells. I would find him on his knees leaning into the rear fender of a small car parked next to a tall SUV or minivan, so he could not be seen. Gasoline buzzes and blitzes, free of charge.

On a sunny Sunday afternoon, I found him in one of his standard locations. The lot was full, compliments of a Blue Jays matinee home game. But he was not just breathing in the gas fumes. To my horror, his mouth was wrapped around the fueling intake of a grey station wagon.

"Doogan, no!" I hollered.

He stopped, looked up at me, and then dropped to the ground weeping. He wept uncontrollably. I sat beside the front fender and waited, while he lay at the back.

Finally he dragged his body into a sitting position, his eyes rolling back into his head as he slurred his words, "Okay, okay, that's it. No more. Okay, I promise."

I told him he had crossed far enough into the danger zone that he had to let me call for help. Within weeks, Doogan had lost entire portions of his mind. Often, he could not remember where he had left his belongings or what my name was or even where he was. I pleaded with him, while he pleaded back that I just leave him alone. As we yelped at each other, he slid his leg out from the shade of the back bumper and into the sunlight shining between the vehicles. Then he began raising his foot and tapping his toe back to where his heel had been on the ground.

"I just can't catch it. Damn it. Just once," he barked.

And there it was. Perhaps the one and only game played by children in every part of the world: Shadow Jumping. No rules. No equipment. Just a bit of daylight required. Racing in circles trying to jump on someone's shadow while jumping away from their efforts to pounce on yours. The only real frustration is that you can never catch your own.

Shadow Jumping

I recall shadow jumping in the elementary school yard in Weston. A harmless bit of fun trying to cross between the sun and friends' shadows while keeping my own shadow angled away from their eager leaps. It was fun with my good buddies, but the game changed when kids who were not my friends joined in. The innocent laughter sharpened with uninvited jabs like, "Ha! Right on your head! Ha! Right in the guts! Ha! You're dead!" Said in malicious tones that broke the spirit of happiness down the centre, and always just made me want to quit.

While the rest of his peers outgrew the game, Doogan never did. It became his own little quirk, and a way to pass the time. A game he could never win, no matter how many times he tried. And still, always, he did try.

What an extraordinary outward display of the inside of the boy. One not so far from all of us, I imagine.

Doogan was a boy who had known only too well what it felt like to have someone else's foot pin down his head and guts. He knew what it felt like to have people stomp on his image with contempt and malice. And all he was looking for was one opportunity to get a foothold on his own image. So he chased the opportunity through his young life, out on to the streets, and into the fumes. Never giving up on attempts to capture everything wrapped up inside his own silhouette.

"I have to get you to real help. You are going to die doing this," I pleaded.

"Never! No one can see! No one can know!" He wobbled to his feet and ran away, bouncing between cars as he worked to maintain his balance.

As the weeks rattled by, he became more and more difficult to find. And when I did, he was almost always hooked up with a new batch of people. Ones I recognized, but did not know. All I knew was that they were not living on the streets, but were pimping it with the most unforgiving chemicals and concoctions available. Doogan began doing what's called muling for another group of maniacal shadow jumpers. Quite simply, for Doogan that meant taking on the risk of delivering drugs for pushers to other addicts and receiving some chemical stash as payment. Dealers with only one bottom line: nobody else matters. Not street guys looking to get by, but drive-by controllers working the "losers" who would do anything for a small rock, quick snort or fleeting fix.

Soon after, I could not find Doogan anywhere. I checked out all his old haunts, from the back corners of parking lots to the ravine he blazed up in, but he was nowhere to be found. Days into his absence I crossed a line and quizzed a main dealer.

"Your boy is likely dead," he sneered, and continued, "West coast last I heard. But no way his sorry ass made it all the way." And that was that. He spat, turned and walked away.

Months later, while out west for a speaking engagement, I took a day to walk through Vancouver's volatile east end. It is a sad and personal tour I take whenever I am there, but this time I was on a scavenger hunt. Part of me wanted to find him. Part of me didn't. Not knowing always makes it easier to imagine a miracle. But every good street worker learns to bet against his or her better judgement at some point.

I wandered for hours through the horrors of the beautiful city's ignored blight. A festering village inside a great metropolis tragically in need of good medicine, social physicians and spiritual healing. Streets and alleys filled with damaged shadow jumpers who can no longer participate in the game.

I had all but given up and was approaching the other-worldliness of the city's lovely tourist section, called Gastown, when I noticed a long leg stretched out from between a group of people squatting against a wall. A tapping, toe back to heel, toe back to heel.

Doogan, looking like the poster child for death before death. Habitually trying to step on his own shadow. Sitting between two crusty old men. All three of them with bent coffee cups in front of them, panning for change. I recalled his words: "The only thing worse than a murderer...."

I kneeled in front of him and spoke his name softly. But he did not answer or respond in any way. His eyes rolled in his head and drool fell from his chin. He was gone.

You can blame toxins, fumes and venoms. You can accuse the dealers and poison puppeteers. But at the end of the day, when all the finger pointing is over, the fault really always belongs to the ones who start it all by breaking hearts, abusing souls, mistreating love—and shadow jumping cruelly.

Doogan did not understand me. He would not let me lead him away. His brain was fried and his body was racing to catch up. His face was blue with bruises. His arms were purple and covered in needle tracks. He reeked of urine and vomit. And one thing was sure: he would not be back when he made something of himself.

I had passed a couple of inner-city street emergency workers blocks back, so I returned to find them and told them Doogan's story. With exhausted and empty eyes they listened and nodded. With kind but unpromising tones they agreed to look out for him. I recognized the sad look on their patient and tired faces—the look that comes when one tries to build sandcastles one grain at a time.

I returned to Doogan one last time. He was barely present while begging at the threshold between downtown Vancouver's scourge and its delight, as people passed him by. None would imagine a bright and handsome boy, well-dressed, well-educated, from great wealth and with too much pride to look anything but his best. I put five dollars in his cup and tried to pray. But I could not. I did not know what to pray for, and I couldn't find the strength to try. My faith was too small to believe in the size of miracle required. I was afraid to ask for what I really wanted, which was for the life-giver to bring death. And I was too grieved to frame death as "new life." So I sat at his feet and just watched him. I cursed his parents and looked scornfully at every apparently well-adjusted person who walked by. But the distraction of my anger wore thin quickly. Finally I simply reached down and put my hands on Doogan's tapping foot and held it still with both hands. In that moment my prayer came. That whatever it looked like, God would give him rest. Just rest. I released my hands and his foot fell sideways. No more tapping toe to heel, in search of his own shadow. For me it was a bent, almost unrecognizable hope to see a boy who had lost his mind sitting still for a few moments.

Can parents be forgiven for inflicting catastrophic abuses on their children?

The ridiculous truth is "yes." By stitching complete repentance to a renewing faith authentically before God, girded by his grace, yes.

But that is God. The creator of the sun, moon and stars. The Alpha and Omega.

It is not me. Not yet. And, I am guessing, not in this lifetime.

December 2004

For northern cities that rest against large bodies of water, global warming and what is known as "lake effect" can summon their own unique brand of winter chaos. Weather that doesn't just slow a frenzied city, but that shuts it down completely. This was one of those nights.

The freezing rain fell like tiny metal darts, like angry chimes bouncing off awnings, parked cars and glazed roadways. Everything was miserable, grey and cold. Even the measured movement of hooded strangers on lower Jarvis Street seemed extra miserable, grey and cold. Flickering Christmas lights strung carelessly through the security bars of closed dollar stores were dulled by onion layers of ice forming on grimy windowpanes. Those with nowhere to be, or with no one waiting, cocooned themselves in darkened doorways, waiting as always for time to stop standing still.

The streets were heavy with the peculiar weight of scarcity—scarcity of comfort and warmth, of joy and anticipation, and most of all, the tragic scarcity of belonging.

I had journeyed for some time through the elements, marveling at the injustice of it all for those stuck in it with no reprieve. After an hour of skidding from iced street to iced street, I came upon a disturbing sight. Beneath the dim yellow glow of an ancient streetlight was a young woman sitting in an abandoned parking lot. Unlike others out on this night who would be rolled in a frigid ball or bundled, she was leaning against a six-inch cement parking curb, legs extended, swaying back and forth with her face to the sky, accepting the quick ice pellets as punishment. She was weeping and scolding herself. A very stern scolding.

I kept a healthy distance at first. I did not know her. Best said, even now, I truly do not know her. But the time, place and her total abandonment of self-consciousness raised my suspicions. She seemed too coherent to be stoned. No slur of inebriation. Quite young and too deliberate in speech to be suffering mental illness. No. Something else.

A stuck thinker, thinking.

Yes. Stuck and thinking. A brutal place to be. Not a place earmarked solely for those who are homeless, by any means. Not one exclusively for those waiting in prison cells or hiding from the law. A place that everyone finds themselves at some point. In fact, this sweet one's distress reminded me more of a single mom at the kitchen table in a small apartment late at night, surrounded by bills she cannot pay, replaying the dreams of her college years and wondering how it all went wrong. Or of a wealthy executive sitting at his desk in the corner office, wondering why his teenage children have rejected him. The kind of stuck that forces a mind to beg, wish and plead to turn back the hands of time. Calling, like children who messed up their turn in a game, to do it over.

Even still, sometimes there can be a special kind of "stuck": a form of denial that works for you, instead of against you. The seldom spoken of, and hard to identify, "healthy" version of denial. The dreamlike edition that allows someone to believe they can still get un-stuck if they relentlessly question what has occurred and keep moving forward while doing so. The "Did that really just happen? Oh no, it couldn't have!" kind that was bearing down on this young one as she replayed the day in her head, oblivious to all else.

She was so focused on sorting out her stuck-ness that she did not notice me. Or just didn't care. However, after several minutes of listening in on her intimate soliloquy, I began to feel uncomfortable receiving and gluing together the sordid details of her story, without her permission.

I took three or four cautious steps towards her. I leaned forward a tiny bit, set my business card at her side, stepped back and simply said, "Can I help you?"

She swayed a bit slower, looked down at the card, then back into the sky. Ice pellets bounced off her forehead.

"Never again," she nodded evenly. "Never again."

She repeated it over and over. Soon after, two-word sentences became lengthy sentences. Eventually, an uncertain distance between us became a safe distance. And a frightened girl spoke more assuredly with each passing moment, until the voice of a bright, attentive young woman filled the air.

She was dressed ambitiously, but her style and allure was ruined in the unforgiving sleet. Accented now in items she scrounged at an army-surplus store after everything fell apart, she was an image of overwhelming disappointment. All the tragic signs of a dreamer's plan gone wrong. Very wrong.

Eighteen-year-old Iris left a terrifying home on the prairies, making her way to Toronto to answer an ad that simply read: "Young models: no experience required." She used all she had on travel fare and an off-the-rack outfit. But the end result was vicious. She wouldn't get stoned and she wouldn't get naked. And models were not what they were looking for. She escaped through the bathroom window of a dingy hideaway porn studio.

The web of lies spun with promises of fame and fortune by sexual predators is astounding. Ugly, sticky and terrifying. There are few lies as costly or vile as these. Lies that can steal the bodies and souls of children and youth in the blink of an eye and twist the life out of them so effortlessly. Countless young people hike down the same yellow brick road as Iris did, only to find there is no wonderful wizard at the end, and there is much, much worse than the wicked witch. Two-sentence ads and thirty-second phone calls promising bright lights and endless adulation are, more often than not, the bear traps that snare tiny, innocent creatures just wandering by. Pimps who call themselves agents. Cameras feeding live images to fiends trapped by their own inhuman perversion. Sedatives for nervous newcomers that paralyze their conscious state and introduce lifelong addictions. Rape. Threats. Manipulation. Altered states. Gang bangs. Brainwashing. Beatings. Human trafficking. These are just a few of the nouns. The detailed verbs and adjectives that go with them are unfathomable. The only promise kept is one from the advertisement that didn't mean what you thought it would mean: "The possibilities are endless."

She took a closer look at my business card, holding it between the index finger and thumb of oversized green workgloves. Fat-fingered gloves designed for construction workers, with black leather thumbs and piping along the knuckles.

"Youth Unlimited? Tim Huff?" She read it like someone might read a name out of the phone book, as if to say "so what." Indeed, I had read my name on that same business card many a time and asked the same question.

Chapter 19

But she gave me a chance. It was either God's great intervention that she would dare to give me the time of day—a male stranger walking the streets at night—or a state of complete shock and overwhelming naiveté. My best guess is that it was all of these.

Minute by minute she transformed. It was brilliant to behold. Like a magic trick that you cannot believe is happening right before your eyes. She started to speak with an extraordinary determination. She insisted on writing an IOU rather than "just accepting charity," if I would simply help her get a ticket east to her grandma's. It could all be worked out! Life re-jigged, no-nonsense new-ness, the day washed away, and most of all, unstuck—if she could just get to grandma's.

I cannot begin to count the number of grandmas and grandpas I have known who have turned in award-winning performances as guardian angels in the lives of young people needing home. I believe with all my heart that God has something extra special for them in heaven. Some glorious place of honour for teary-eyed grandmothers who sat in courtrooms with their pierced and tattooed grandsons before them in handcuffs—while their friends went on cruises and sightseeing bus trips. Grandfathers who faith-fully took their pregnant teenage granddaughters to doctor appointments without giving a single lecture—while their friends went south for the winter or met at the coffee shop to talk about the good ol' days. Grandparents who survived economic crises, world wars, life-threatening diseases, jobs they hated that put food on the table, deaths, and disappointments too great to speak aloud. Dreaming of getting to retirement healthy enough to enjoy a simpler life—only to be called back into the grind. This time with older and slower bodies. This time with weary souls and fatigued minds. This time facing not just age gaps, but unimaginable cultural gaps. Light years away from simply going to see a grandson's little league game or a grand-daughter's music recital before going home for afternoon tea and a nap. Grandmas and grandpas living out their golden years as moms and dads to two, and sometimes three, generations of dependents. The beautiful, silent and truest heroes of our time. And whether the rest of the world sees it or not, God surely does.

The next 90 minutes were a whirlwind. The complexities of her history, her ambitions and the certainty that many things would happen "NEVER AGAIN" were enormous.

Ninety minutes later, Iris was waving goodbye through the frosted win-dows of a long-journey bus, on a thoughtful and timely ride east.

Soaking wet. Determined smile. And a big green work glove waving a confident goodbye.

A few days later I bought a Christmas tree at a corner lot. It was late, and the workers were tired and cold. I paid my cash to one worker in winter coveralls, while another one put a fresh cut on the stump.

"Can I carry this out to your vehicle for you?" he asked.

"Nope, I got it. Thanks."

I reached into the big pockets in my coat and pulled out my work gloves, readying to lug the wide balsam fir to my truck. As I bent over to lift the tree, I stopped and stared at the palm of my left hand. Then my right. My gloves were blue. But in every other way they were just like the ones Iris wore, with black leather thumbs and piping on the knuckles. My eyes welled up.

"Um...are you okay, buddy?" the workers asked awkwardly.

Looking down at my hands, I clenched my grip and heard the voice of a broken little girl becoming a victorious woman. In a clear, soulful voice, "Never again."

I cleared my throat and worked at mustering up my best guy voice as I wiped my eyes with the knuckles of one of the gloves. "Ya, it's all good. No big deal. See ya." I reached between the boughs and trudged away.

The 19th-century French poet Victor Hugo said, "Have courage for the great sorrows in life, and patience for the small ones. When you have laboriously accomplished your daily tasks, go to sleep in peace. God is awake."

I had worn those work gloves for countless daily tasks. Shoveling snow, yard work and small household projects. Iris had worn hers for the tasks of courage and survival. Tasks of the soul. And so it is: while one inspects and chooses the freshest fruit from the produce aisle, another just down the street seeks out edible scraps from a trash bin. Both tending to their tasks for the day. While one races from store to store shopping for trendy footwear, another, just outside that very store, lines sole-less boots with newspaper. Both tending to their tasks for the day. And while one, still as much a child as a woman, travels alone across the country searching for someone who will value her without hurting her, another tries to decide which side of the Christmas tree looks fullest and which side should face the wall. Both tending to their tasks for the day. No matter how we reconcile, justify or ignore what the value and cost of our tasks may be—whether we truly find peace, or shamelessly "make peace" with the great discrepancies we allow—one glorious and terrifying truth is sure, just as the great poet assured: "God is awake."

Chapter 19

A month after meeting Iris, a small envelope with no return address arrived in the mail. In it was cash. Just a bit more than the bus fare east, along with my own crumpled business card. Written on the back:

"Thank you. Never again. Iris."

May 1996

In 1967, the Beatles were asked to write a song and perform it on the first-ever live worldwide television event. A two-hour program simultaneously broadcast to twenty-six countries around the globe, simply called "Our World." They were asked to pen something that could be understood by any person, anywhere, and in any language. The end result was the classic hit "All You Need Is Love."

While a global audience of young music lovers and Beatles fans embraced the song as a mantra for their generation, many a parent chastised the sensibility of having young people buy into anything so trite and make-believe.

Nearly two decades later, I met the one kid whose entire life could be summed up in the five words of that Fab Four title.

Desmond.

"You get paid to like us." Desmond had no idea how dark his words were in contrast to the luminous spring afternoon. He and I were sitting with three others in a parkette just off the Yonge Street strip when he landed this sinister quip.

All kinds of responses bobbed around in my brain, as the small scruffy group awaited my reply. Godly responses like I knew I was supposed to give.

Technical responses about gracious donors who make it all possible and living on a "faith support" salary. Even laid-back hippie-esque responses that would have floated nicely into a sixties-era Beatles theme. But Desmond had a way of sucking the life out of me that, on this day, left nothing more than the strength to spit out cruelly, "Then I don't get paid enough."

They all laughed, thinking I was joking. For the other three, it was a joke, but for Desmond, I confess it was true.

In the messy world of runaways and throwaways that I adore, Desmond was my own personal keep-away.

Street terms are always changing. Some hold esteem and validation as street credibility, while others attach instant and irrepressible stigma. While they mean nothing to the general population, they mean a great deal to a street population that in many ways polices itself.

While they represent the smallest fraction of the street population, "twinkies" and "weekend warriors" are not well received. These are the unfair stereotypes of street kids: brats and rebellious ingrates who just don't like the rules at home. They pop up on the streets as fair-weather rebels, but a country like Canada does not see much of them outside of the warm weather months. At least not for very long.

Likewise, there is an entire population of couch-surfers and shelter-hoppers who are only one bad day away from sleeping under the stars and through the elements. A mixed bag of young people: some fleeing abuse, some trying to prove themselves, some paying back neglect with worry, some chasing addictions, and some acting like spoiled brats. While my experience has been dominated by young people with dreadful parents, this is certainly not always the case. I regularly get photos and phone calls from all across North America from loving parents who are worried sick, asking me to watch out for their child, and to call immediately if I find them. Parents of all kinds of prodigal sons and daughters, who felt their children gave them no choice but to move from tough love to tough consequences. While these young ones tend not to hide on the streets the same way as those I have spent most of my street time with, no kid who reaches the streets is ever free of danger.

One of the most shortsighted notions of street work is that we should only invest in the ones who "deserve" our help. While it takes a great deal of discretion to do and say the right thing, we cannot afford to dismiss any young person on the streets, regardless of why they are there. The pimps, pushers, gangs, muggers, cults, pedophiles and predators could care less about the "whys." They are just glad to meet them, greet them, steal them and use them.

The street will eat anyone. A rich kid goes down the gullet the same as a poor one. A young person with a great mom or dad can get chewed up the same as one without.

There are often two telltale signs of a young person who is simply playing out rebellion on the streets. One is that they overact their toughness. The other is that they say little about why they are out there, or anything at all, hoping the hardcore street population will just assume it's a dire reason. Sidestepping even the simplest questions, like "where are you from" can be quite telling. It is part of an attempt to mimic the first noticeable thing about hardcore street life—the idea that I belong on the streets because I don't belong anywhere else.

Not Desmond. From square one, he would routinely spew out stuff that endeared him to no one.

"I'm just out here to make my old lady sick and make my dad squirm."

"I'm not a loser like everyone else out here—I can go back anytime I want."

Even the most hardcore seen-it-all kids on the street did not know what to make of him. Desmond was a green alien among the alienated. He would deliberately say vicious things to those he knew had been physically or sexually abused. He goaded the mentally ill, bullied the developmentally challenged, and told old homeless people to just "lie down and die." Desmond could also maintain a vile running commentary on anything sexual. He catcalled every female over the age of 12 who passed him by—the homeless and the home-owners, the cheerleaders and the bookworms, the pony-tailed and the bee-hived. Something uniquely perverse for everyone.

The eventual crackdown on "squeegee-ing" in Toronto occurred as a result of antics such as Desmond's. The 10 percent fixed in the crosshairs of government and media attention. He would spit on the windshields of those who weren't interested and jump in front of cars that would not pay what he thought his efforts were worth. He was renowned in my street circles as the only person to have ever successfully urinated on a moving vehicle from bumper to bumper. While he had the ability to anger and terrify dozens of drivers and passengers every hour, his ability to outrage the other young people and adults who squeegeed—the 90 per cent who did so respectfully and with a smile—was remarkable.

Hate is a strong word. But for many who knew him, it was not strong enough. And dislike just was not even close. Desmond cornered the market on abhorrence with every odious breath he took. For the first time in my life, I felt like I was "getting paid to like someone." Or at least to pretend to. And even with that dumbed-down effort, I was failing miserably.

Chapter 20

From a survival perspective, the street is a thug. Unforgiving and unrepentant. When it comes to hope, it is a desert wasteland: nothing as far as the eye can see, the occasional mirage and a flowered cactus when it's least expected. When it comes to identity, it is a starving animal, willing to consume almost anything to be nourished. And socially it is the most awkward dance partner of all. Turf declarations are tentative at best. External vestibules and alcoves are claimed with wet sleeping bags, dirty looks and tough words. There are no deeds of entitlement or alloy deadbolts to lock. And when it comes to street corners and sidewalks, you bump into whoever you bump into and learn to coexist with the lambs and lions, or you move on to the next street corner and sidewalk. It was in this that Desmond tested a wrath too great.

On a frantic, shopper-happy Saturday afternoon, Desmond languished around the entranceway of the city's downtown retail mega hub, the Eaton Centre. Bumming smokes. Demanding change. Wisecracking strangers. Blurting out racial and homophobic diatribes based on visual stereotypes and assumptions. All in all, it was Desmond just being Desmond.

Two police officers on bicycles were winding their way through the crowd when Desmond called out to them.

"Pigs, pigs, hey pigs! Weed, crack, the whole deal! These guys got it all!" He stood pointing at three bewildered street youth, sitting innocently off to the side.

The police dismounted and marched towards him. All that they had heard clearly was "Pigs!" Thus, Desmond had their full attention. They stood in the middle of a curious crowd for several minutes before they walked over to the wall and told the three teenagers to stand, pull out their pockets and open their bags. The kids stood slowly. Two of them reluctantly began doing as they had been told. But the one refused.

"Why? Why? We ain't doing nothing!" he fumed.

One officer became more forceful, and the third boy became more resistant. And things got ugly. Very ugly, loud and pushy.

The issues of homelessness are like bags of bricks that inner-city police officers are forced to carry. Not simple to work with by any means. Not desired. Annoying, burdensome and distracting. But, carrying them is part of the job. And those who accept them and carry them well are stronger because of it. I have been inspired by several of those officers. "To serve and protect" is a high calling. And while I have known many an officer who has shown extraordinary grace and understanding in serving and protecting all people—with or without homes—the police force is made up of as many mere mortals as any other occupation. Including those who are sick and tired of carrying that bag of bricks. One such officer was in response here.

Within seconds the three teenagers were lined up and spun around. Hands against the plate glass windows, legs spread. Within the crowd gathered near the revolving doors, I could see Desmond, grinning like a gremlin.

I walked over to the officers to offer some perspective, but it was a bad idea. It was not welcome.

"You really wanna be a part of this, buddy?" I was scolded. "You'll be next!"

The other officer put his hand on my shoulder and drew me back, "Just let it go, walk away, and this will all be done in a minute." So, I inched back, waited and watched.

Sure enough, there was no weed or crack. No "the whole deal." Just three bewildered kids who had been people watching from the sidelines, wishing they had enough money to get something in the food court.

The lead officer turned on a dime, red-faced like a fire-breathing dragon. He paced through the crowd hunting for Desmond, while the other cop stayed with the bikes. But Desmond stayed just long enough to watch the final scene, and vanished before the credits.

"The other kid! That one with the mouth! Where the hell is he?" the officer stormed at me.

I shrugged with authentic ignorance, while he brushed by me, furious.

What I did know was what the humiliated kids tucking in their pockets were thinking. I also knew that this story would have legs—street legs that would be faster than Desmond's. And I knew that while the officers felt justice had not been served, the street's own brand of justice would be. Worst of all, in my own ugly way, I was almost glad of it.

Twelve hours later, under a hazy yellow moon, I came across a lump in the middle of Grange Park. Curled beneath a young maple, Desmond was a bloody mess. Both of his eyes were puffed shut and three of his front teeth were gone. And still, even then, I felt paid to like him. He looked pathetic. I was pathetic.

It is perhaps laid out best in *Christianity for Dummies,* authored by Richard Wagner, Chapter One: Good News in a Bad News World. "The God of Christianity is a God of love and holiness. People have always had a hard time trying to grasp the balance between the two, which is why some people tend to focus on holiness and justice and forget love." Me to a tee when it came to Desmond—jacked up for justice, and completely forgetting love.

"Why? Why would you do that? Why do you do these things? What are you thinking?" I asked him, in a cocky tone.

Desmond moaned his way into a sitting position. He sat for the longest time, with his hands holding the sides of his face as though holding all the pieces in place, and said nothing. I asked him again, a bit softer, a bit kinder. And finally tears welled up in his swollen eyes and rolled down his bruised cheeks and over the ends of his cracked lips.

"I don't know," he whispered with a painful lisp. "I don't know."

Desmond had long claimed that he had a glorious home he could go back to any time. Cash in abundance, food pouring out of stainless steel appliances, heated swimming pool, high-tech this, top-of-the-line that. I felt it long past due to call him out on it.

"Let me call home, and let's get you back."

Too pained to debate, agree or disagree, he pulled his dad's crumpled business card from his backpack and handed it to me. Then he lay back down and cried.

Beneath the flickering fluorescent bulb of a vandalized phone booth, I discovered what was at the core, rotting the boy I so hated. The boy I had forgotten to love.

"Hello sir, I am calling about your son."

"Uh-huh. What's he done now?"

"He's hurt."

"Uh. Ya. What's new?" Long sigh. "Probably deserved it." Pause. "Right?"

"Do you want to know where he is, or come and get him?"

"We are on our way to Greece in the morning. We have been planning this vacation for months, and we aren't going to let him spoil it for us. He has a key, he knows the security code, there's lots of food in the fridge. And he damn well knows his own way home."

Click.

Desmond: private schools, beach houses and platinum credit cards. All the advantages with the scales tipped heavily in his favour, long before he could even tie his own shoes. "...Nothing you can say, but you can learn how to play the game...it's easy!"

Desmond: despised, disgraced, defeated, disillusioned, dishonoured. The boy the Beatles unknowingly wrote for: "All You Need Is Love!"

He had everything else.

Somewhere between trying to be perfect and feeling he was never good enough, Desmond did more than simply give up. He launched an assault on everything and everyone that would ever expect anything but the worst from him.

"Your dad said you can come home anytime you want," I said unconvincingly.

"Ya, I bet," he replied, knowing only too well the sorry context of such a statement.

Some of the older and more streetwise kids had speculated that Desmond was either the product of a chronic drug habit with no down time, mentally ill, bipolar, or a loading zone for some or all of the above. Many rumours and assumptions had been sprinkled into the heavy dough of hatred. But none were true. Desmond spent the next three hours telling me his story. Nursing his bloodied gums as he spoke, he used soft tones and dignified language. He spoke intelligently and philosophically. And by the end, I treasured every moment at his side. I told him that his story reminded me of the Beatles' song, "All You Need Is Love." He rolled his eyes in sad and embarrassed agreement.

Somewhere in those precious hours, he revealed God's soulful handiwork to me in ways I had missed. For the boy I had hated was brilliant, thoughtful and sensitive. And most of all, the boy I hated was a master of character disguise, fooling everyone from discovering a boy who should have been esteemed and admired. Loved.

And why? Because more than anything, the boy I hated, hated himself. And while someone actually loving him may have infiltrated that stronghold, I was somehow too weak and cowardly to be the one. I chose to really care about him when I finally liked what I saw and heard. But you don't need a brain, faith, God or an ounce of humanity to like people when they say what you want, do what you want, and are who you want them to be.

Desmond left Toronto, fearing for his life. He had made one too many enemies while living out his tortured and ugly street identity. On the night I last saw him in Toronto, he held up a green bank card and said, "There is just enough left in here to buy me one more start." His words made me feel sick and hopeful at the same time. I felt sick that his upbringing told him that money could buy such things. And hopeful that what he really meant was that his resources would allow him to get somewhere else and give him a fresh chance to be the real Desmond. As author Anna Lappe said: "Hope doesn't come from whether the good news is winning out over the bad. It's simply a choice to take action." Desmond made that choice.

While I prayed for Desmond many months after he left, I spent more time praying that God would forgive me. Of course, he did the first time I asked, so really I had been wasting my time, and his. I imagine nothing irks God more than when he tells us something, like that we are forgiven, and we (at least the so-called "believers") don't believe him. In essence, either questioning his sovereignty or calling him a liar. But foolishly, I do it all the time. And once again I had this familiar feeling in my gut like I needed to suffer through my guilt, not be released of it instantly—and with God seemed the rightest place to do that wrong thing. Though that theology is completely whacked, it felt right at the time. It so often does.

Eventually time spent wondering what happened to Desmond seeped away along with my prayers for him and the God-I'll-do-better-next-time prayers. Out of sight, out of mind: guilt relief 101.

Nearly three years later, I was walking along the shoreline of a beach in Vancouver, 4,500 kilometres west of Toronto. It was a bright day, and the coast was filled with happy people doing happy things. In the distance, there was a hippie-like group sitting in a circle with guitars and hand drums, singing and laughing. As I walked towards them, I was struck by their willingness just to take in the day, to be happy and harmless in the moment. A beautiful place at a beautiful time. As I walked past the group, I made eye contact with a couple of them, smiled in appreciation of their music, and just kept strolling. But when I got three of four steps past them, the music stopped. Mid-song, somewhere along the bridge of Green Day's "When I Come Around."

A new song began with one guitar and one singer.
There's nothing you can do that can't be done.
Nothing you can say that can't be sung.
Nothing you can say but you can learn how to play the game.
It's easy....

I stopped in the sand, frozen by the song and voice. I listened closely for a few seconds with my eyes closed, and turned.

Desmond!

He looked happy and healthy, and most of all, at peace. A postcard image of west coast cool: an earth-toned vest, tight-knit beanie, unstrapped sandals and a tightly trimmed goatee. He smiled at me, larger than life. His friends looked on with curious smiles as he sang loudly and confidently, and I listened in amazement. He did not stop. He just kept on singing, beaming from ear to ear.

He sang his way through the chorus, while his friends joined in: "All you need is love, All you need is love, All you need is love, love...Love is all you need." Then he gave me a thumbs-up between strums, and a nod as if to say, "Here I am. I'm okay. It's okay. Move on, friend." With a secret musical code, he shared the hope he had found and released me from the guilt of my own hypocrisy. It was God's special gift to both of us when we expected it least.

So I moved on, honouring that, indeed, Desmond certainly had.

Can there be hope without love? Perhaps some odd imitation of hope, born out of ambition. The kind of ambition that only some people possess, driving them out of one situation and into the next. But true life-giving hope cannot exist without love. The God of love is never mistaken for the God of ambition.

Despite the absurdity that a rat-raced, high-tech population still believes that "all you need is love," that simple phrase points to a truth spoken by every great spiritual leader in the history of humankind. And of all the texts ever written about love, none is more captivating or inspired than 1 Corinthians 13. Verse 13 of that chapter points to three things that will never be superseded:

"And now these three remain: faith, hope and love. But the greatest of these is love."

Somehow I had forgotten. Thanks to Desmond, I won't again.

It was so dramatic, it was almost like stage acting. Over-exaggerated bawling, with her head tucked between her withered hands. Her shoulders rose and fell six inches with each bellow. Just complete submission to—or terror at—her plight.

It was just before midnight when I came across her. A middle-aged woman plopped on the sidewalk of a railway overpass. An obscure place to be, for sure. Not enough people (especially at this time of night) for any luck at kindness, and not hidden enough for the safety of cover. Curled in a ball, she looked like a large package tossed from a passing car. From a distance, more like a giant bag of garbage.

I kneeled beside her, but before I could say a word she peeked at me from between her fingers and begged, "Please don't hurt me. Please, please don't hurt me." She closed her fingers back across her eyes and continued to sob.

I had never seen hands so dirty or beaten in all of my life. They seemed blackened with the grime of centuries. Her fingernails were long and green and chipped apart. Worst of all, her hands looked so sore. While I couldn't see her palms, the backs were crusty and the heels of her hands were swollen and raw. These were the hands of unthinkable pain and unimaginable survival. The grotesque hands of an uncelebrated survivor.

Chapter 21

"Oh, I won't hurt you, I promise," I said. "But can we get you somewhere safe?"

"No! No! They're going to beat me up!"

I sat high on both knees and looked around. No one in sight. But as I looked left to right I realized her keen survival tactics. She had positioned herself in the one place where she could see everyone and everything coming. The overpass was well-lit by streetlights. The drop behind the rails she sat against was a good ten metres, and the opposing sidewalk was four lanes of traffic away. So, there would be no threat from front or back. Sitting at the centre of the bridge, she had the advantage of at least thirty metres on either side to see what, or who, was coming at any given time. What had seemed an obscure location at first glance was in fact very deliberate.

There is a certain indefinable ring to the voices of street women who are challenged by mental illness. Part volume, part tone and part cadence—all just a measure off the norm. In addition, hers had an extra gauge of fear to notch up that volume, put an extra bend on that tone and quicken that cadence.

"The big girls. Those big ones. They said I stole it. But I didn't, I really didn't! And now they is gonna beat me up." She broke back into wailing.

And so goes the spinning and cruel world of street psychiatrics. Dunking your head into stories that are life-and-death one moment and in another orbit the next. Perhaps the hardest place to know how to help, and how to hope for someone, is here in the fen of information that is only partly comprehendible, partly sensible and often only part reality. And still, regardless of my assessment, or even what was true or not, she was stuck in the terror of her own world. For her, the fear was very real.

I reached out and took her hand, "Then what can we do here to make things better?"

She stopped crying, stopped talking, and all but stopped breathing. She stared at my hand on hers as though an alien had touched her. Just gazing at my clean hand on hers. Her mouth was wide open, and her tongue dropped over her gums, where all but a couple of teeth were missing. Just as a tear fell from her chin onto my hand, she lowered her other hand on mine.

She lifted my hand and held it beneath her chin and began to rock back and forth. Slowly. Gently. Like a mother rocks her newborn.

Not a stroke of genius. Not the experience of years on the street. Nothing intentional or insightful. And certainly, not anything that could not have come from anyone. Just the touch of a hand in a bewildering moment.

She cooed in the tiniest of voices, "I like holding your hand."

I smiled back, "Ya, me too."

I could feel the calluses on her palms and thick broken layers of skin poking between the bends in her fingers. Here, at close range, the stench of her breath was almost suffocating, and I could see grease and gravel in her hair. And still, the warmth of the moment was almost heavenly.

There are endless studies that prove that human touch alone can impact life in a way medical science never can. From the moment of birth, there is no instinct more innate than touch. From laboratory scientists to pediatric nurses, it is a proven fact and sworn truth.

I was fortunate enough to learn it early. While paying my way through college, I worked evenings and weekends at a pilot project group home for what were then known as "the most medically fragile and developmentally challenged people in a home setting" (meaning not in an institution or hospital setting). None of them walked or talked. When we were not feeding them (often through tubes), changing them and cleaning them, most of our time was spent tugging, rolling and pressing them through range-of-motion exercises. Two of the five residents did not respond in any way to light, movement, temperature, taste, smell or sound. But those same ones always, and only, smiled when their cheeks or the palms of their hands were rubbed. At 19 years of age, it was the most life-changing experience I had ever known. I learned about touch in a way that a million scientific documents could not have taught.

The greatest curse of our time is that touch has been stolen from us. Or more accurately, that we have allowed it to be stolen from us. Too many perverts. Too many predators. Too many abusers. Too many cowards. And too many lawsuits.

If our world withers and dies without war, it will surely be because we surrendered the godly beauty of innocent touch. Outstretched hands of peace and tenderness. Open hands of surrender. And resting hands of assurance. The wordless reminder that we are all connected. The only global language of humanity. Unschooled and unrehearsed responses for a frightened world.

For ten minutes, with eyes closed tightly, she rocked in silence, holding my hand beneath her chin. My legs fell asleep from the knees down, and I could no longer feel my feet. Whenever I began to squirm, just to get a bit more comfortable, she squeezed my hand harder, gave it a tug, and held it tighter against her neck, as if to tell me to "stay still."

Finally she opened her eyes. "Okay. I am going to sleep now."

She rolled to her side, still clutching my hand, and said, "You be the lookout, Okay?"

No discussion. No questions. A done deal all worked out and settled in her mind.

This too has been my experience among survivors such as this. There are only two sets of people in the world: those who will protect you and those who will hurt you. Knowing the difference is the result of calculated guesses and a bizarre bit of discernment based on whatever is trapped in one's mind. Many have been terrified of me because I look like someone who hurt them 20 years before. Others have scooped me up because I reminded them of someone dear from 30 years ago. Confused, absent and chemically altered minds have mistaken me for everyone from John Lennon's ghost to Count Dracula. One of my challenges on the street has been not bursting out laughing in the face of someone who says something ridiculous but believes it in their mind.

Sure enough, she was asleep in an instant. Sucking in large breaths of oxygen and exhaling with the same quiver as a child after a temper tantrum. All the while, my hand was buried between hers. It was one of my great "how did this happen, I must look like a maniac, what am I gonna do now" moments.

But finally my body made the decision for me. The tingling numbness from my crushed legs had traveled to my hips, and I just had to squirm free. Slowly I began to draw my hand out of hers. But each time it was almost loose, she would clutch it tightly and yank it back. So I twisted my wrist and slid to one side, so that only my fingers were squeezed in her hands, and I was able to sit properly and rest my back against the railing.

Common sense told me she was fast asleep, seemingly safe, and it was time to take my leave. She had slept on these streets for an eternity and awakened every morning. But her non-negotiable assignment would not release me. I was "the lookout." I had been charged with an important job and commissioned with a great responsibility.

So I just sat there. Half overachieving idiot, half underachieving guardian angel. Blurred roles, as has always been my specialty.

At two o'clock in the morning, her grip loosened and my sweaty hand was free. But I was not. I had to watch for "The big girls. Those big ones." Sigh. I just wanted her to know one night of protected rest.

In my own late-night stupor I began meditating on a verse I have always adored—the gentle words of Jesus found in Matthew 11:28(NASB): "Come to Me, all who are weary and heavy-laden, and I will give you rest." I prayed that God would grant her godly rest, for just this one night if nothing else, for her body, mind and spirit. That her sore hands, raw gums and soiled body would be soothed. That her racing mind would escape from "the big girls" and all the other worries that snuck up on her. And that her spirit, which could only be understood by the creator, would be calm.

Of course, any time of the day is a good time to pray for people who are homeless. But at no time are deliberate prayers more needed than in the middle of the night, in the dark hours when fear creeps up on even the bravest, when loneliness smothers the most confident, and when hope is most bent.

By four o'clock, I was already an hour into nodding in and out of slumber. And just when I felt I might truly fall into an upright snooze, she began to talk in her sleep.

"It's okay. It's okay, dear. Mommy is right here."

My eyes popped wide open, and I stared at her. Her voice had changed completely. She sounded young and beautiful. Confident, elegant.

"Yes, Mommy is right here, sweetheart."

Could it be? How could it be? Someone's mother? But how? How did it all come to this?

She continued on for some time, dreaming of another time and place, transported to a glorious chapter of life when she was young. Her bright mind was filled with dreams and plans, and her own precious offspring was warm in her arms.

Then she rolled over and was silent again.

But I was wide awake, filled with wonder and awe and tortured by the mystery of her lost story. As twilight tiptoed in, I gazed at her and tried to comprehend the maniacal jabs and knocks of life that stole her blessings and left her so broken. It was all inconceivable.

By six o'clock I heard the traffic sounds of early risers. The business and high-finance early birds getting a jump on catching the commerce worms.

She began to toss and turn. She coughed and sputtered and stretched a long creaky stretch. I sat straight up, proud and prepared. I had done it! I had been part of the one great protected night. The stalwart lookout who remained at his post. I waited with anticipation for her eyes to open and for her to know I had been faithful. To thank me with a smile or a few sweet and confused words of appreciation.

After several frustrating attempts at consciousness, she finally rolled onto her belly and forced her way onto her knees. I waited on a few beautiful, simple and profound words that would inspire me for years to come. She rubbed her eyes over and over, not yet even noticing me. Finally, after a few more shuffles and adjustments, she tipped her head up and looked me square in the eye. My moment had come.

And with a loud morning cackle I will never forget, she tilted her head to one side as though she had no clue who I was or that she had ever met me before and chirped, "What are you doing here?"

Through a long night of profound moments and surprises, she touched my soul without even knowing it.

One great lesson relearned: pride has no place in compassion.

One great gift received: I met someone's long-lost mommy.

Now that is a good night.

September 1987

There is no expression I hear more from sympathizers and supporters than this: "But for the grace of God, go I."

While I always appreciate the thanksgiving and humility in the sentiment, and while it is often accompanied by a charitable act or words of encouragement, something about it makes me uncomfortable. It just feels wrong.

I cannot find the justice in it. What could I have possibly done to receive the gift of a loving safety net of people, while others miss out? To be born with the unjust advantages of being a white male in North America? To enter the world as a healthy baby and grow into adulthood disease-free? The list of "why me's" is endless. But is that grace?

I believe that thanksgiving for one's blessings is crucial. Spiritually, it is paramount to my faith. But even beyond that, for anyone at all, I believe the awareness of blessing, good fortune, dumb luck or whatever people may call it is a moral and ethical must.

And still, that sentence leaves me unsettled. It feels as though there is an awkward suggestion that God's grace is extended to some but not all. And in varying portions. If so, I have no interest in that God.

Even as a child growing up in a church-going family, I sensed something wrong in the sentiment, whenever I heard the words spoken.

I grew up making mischief along the Humber River. I knew the geography of the Weston ravine: the best place to climb trees, the deepest current, where people get mugged most, the family section, hideaways for couples, drug nooks and secret fire pits. In my early years, when I was working with young people in the Weston area, this knowledge was a great advantage.

And while inexperience was my greatest downfall (young twenties, working solo), it was perhaps also my greatest strength. I felt more like a peer to the teenagers and young adults I met than anything else. I had no meetings to attend. No speaking engagements. No reputation to maintain. And not much of a clue about much.

I just wandered haphazardly along the back alleyways, train tracks and river bends I knew so well and looked for young people who looked lost. Procedures, rules, policies and guidelines were not nearly what they are now, and I was more than happy to take advantage of the gaps and question marks.

One Monday morning, I passed by one of Weston's greatest shrines: its hockey arena. One of Toronto's original indoor rinks, with great wooden rafters and bleachers on both sides. No hockey enthusiast enters or leaves without saying "They don't make 'em like this anymore."

As I walked through the arena parking lot, I spotted an unlikely sight. A boy, no more than fifteen years old, poked his head out of the Zamboni entrance, slipped out and headed towards the river. It was a school day, and the arena was technically closed.

He had a two-minute lead on me, but I followed at an even pace. By the time I reached him, he was shoeless and ankle-deep, flipping rocks in the shallow stream.

He spotted me, nodded, and went back to flipping rocks. He couldn't have cared less about who I was or what I was doing.

When I walked towards him, he sighed. "I got no money, and I ain't looking to buy."

"Good, 'cause I ain't selling."

He looked at me as if to say: good, then go away.

Sneaking out of the closed hockey arena, two minutes from the high school—there were lots of questions I could ask, but I skipped over the obvious ones and went with my kid side.

"They're easier to catch at night," I said.

He looked at me with mild interest.

"Ya. We used to come with flashlights," I continued. "The big ones come out from beneath the rocks when it's dark."

Crayfish. Crawfish. Craw daddies. More than five hundred species of these miniature lobsters live in North America alone. I had spent countless hours as a boy catching them along the Humber, scooping them into anything I could find from the nearby trashcan, competing with buddies for numbers and size, and releasing them at the end of the day. As a boy I spent most of July and August with pincer cuts on the thumb and forefinger of my right hand.

He dipped his hand in the water and stood straight. He lifted a soft-skinned, moulting three-incher and said viciously, "Ya. Well this one's getting screwed over in the daytime."

He held its curling body upside down, and with great precision tore off its claws and threw it back into the water. Defenseless prey for turtles and raccoons. He carried the pincers to the shore and dropped them in a beer bottle. He lifted the bottle and shook it at me. It was half-filled with crayfish claws. Dozens and dozens of them.

His name was Dez. More than 15 group home and foster home experiences from his parents, he was supposed to be starting the new school year with yet another "bunch of complete strangers," as he called them. But he only made it through one day of school before giving up. For the first two weeks after Labour Day he simply hid in the cracks of the Weston community and made up his own version of therapy.

"Wow, that's a whole lot of hurt in that bottle," I said.

"Damn right, and if you don't like it, then f**k off," he scoffed and marched back into the water.

I sat on a fallen tree beside the bottle. For two hours I just sat and talked with him. All the while, he caught crayfish after crayfish, ripped apart their only defenses, and bottled them to remember it. I spoke with him about anything and everything that he would allow, but never once spoke about the crayfish again.

I had no idea what I was doing, or what I was supposed to do. I just knew that as long as I did not rock his boat, pass judgement or have any advice to pawn, that I could have this special opportunity to be with a boy that no one else was with.

Tuesday. Wednesday. Thursday. I met him at the river bend behind the hockey arena every morning, talked about his world, and watched him torture crustaceans. I felt responsible to everyone—the school, the truancy department, his group home, the police, my organization, my supervisor, even the humane society, and for sure, a whole whack of baby crayfish wondering why mommy wasn't catching any food. The guilt was ridiculous. And still, to all of them I remained silent, knowing that anything but this would betray the confidence of a boy who had known nothing but betrayal.

Finally on the Thursday he said, "Well, tomorrow is it."

He went on, "They're sending me somewhere else. Some home outside of the city. Whatever. Who cares? Won't last."

Then he held a crayfish with one pincer in his left hand and the other in his right. He yanked simultaneously in separate directions, ripping off both claws at once while the body dropped into the stream. I winced. He noticed, tilted his head and smiled.

Over those four days I watched as at least one hundred crayfish had their lives derailed, simply by being under the wrong rock at the wrong time. If they had been soul-filled creatures, I wonder if the healthy and whole ones that they met beneath the flat stones would have looked at them and said, "but for the grace of God...."

On the final day, the Friday morning, Dez told me about his mom's boyfriend on the first week he moved into their home. Five-year-old Dez told his mom's live-in lover that he hated him, because he was so cruel to him. The man told Dez that if he talked like s**t, he should have his mouth cleaned out in the appropriate place. So he held Dez by the ankles with his head in the toilet, while his mom laughingly flushed it over and over again. And so went his childhood.

I thought back to my own childhood. When I was five years old, my dad taught me how to play softball. When I was five years old, my mom taught me how to make peanut butter cookies. But for the grace of God?

Grace, as I understand it, is God's unmerited favour. I don't have to look in the mirror very long to recognize this is so. But I cannot believe that grace is selectively poured out in any predetermined or predestined way, through blind luck or anything else. Especially when I think about a little boy with his head shoved into the toilet. Surely it is right here, in the atrocities of life, that we need to understand or at least wrestle with grace the most.

Grace is part of the character of God the creator. And because of that, the marvelous calling of humankind is to grow in likeness to the character of God. That our hands, voices, thoughts and actions can project grace. And that we can act and exist in a spirit of grace even when we don't know what to do or say. Reshaping the statement to say: "But for the grace of God can I extend the grace of God."

Inherent in this statement is the removal of pride. Erasing the assumption that I was chosen over another to receive God's grace. Humility is needed to let grace breathe. It is where actual words and tasks are not nearly as important as the way in which they are delivered and carried out. The soft and renewing tone of grace found in the old saying: People may not remember what you say, or what you do. But they will remember how you made them feel. Grace is written all over this truth.

By Friday at noon, there were three beer bottles lined up at the shore, filled with crayfish claws. And it was time to say goodbye. Next town. Next school. Next bunch of total strangers. My voice quivered as I tried to speak about "new beginnings." My inexperience and naiveté were extraordinary. I wanted to say the right youth-worker thing. Dez had enough grace to bite his tongue and let me give it my best shot. I did a dreadful job of it. Just plain awful. I made the beautiful truth sound like drivel, ending with something mindless like "well tomorrow's another day." Ugh.

Dez stood with the water up to his knees listening to me. Very patient. Very long-suffering. We both endured a good thick dose of me. But I could tell he had something to say. So I finally shut up.

We had talked for hours, five days in a row, and I am quite sure that nothing I had said meant a thing to him in the context of his hurting world. But in the final moments, it was back to square one that he wanted to go.

He held up a remarkably large crayfish at eye level. It was the biggest one I had seen him pluck from the riverbed all week, its pincers bent forward like praying hands. And for the first time he really stopped to look at it, gazing from side to side, top to bottom. He seemed shocked by the extraordinary complexity of its exoskeleton. So many caught and crippled, but until now, he had never noticed. It was profoundly similar to his own existence, and that of all the young people just like him surviving day to day. Lives that require time and interest to be appreciated and celebrated.

"Why are they easier to catch at night?" he asked.

"Huh? Well, um..." I stuttered, as I recalled telling him that on the first day I met him.

Defeated, I said, "I guess they feel safer...y'know, from predators."

He looked over at the bottles and closed his eyes. When he opened them, they were red and watery. He leaned over and placed the crayfish at the bottom of the river. No torture, no tossing, no deposit to a beer bottle.

He just stood straight and sighed, "Ya. I get that."

But for the grace of God, go any of us.

Go all of us.

August 2006

I hadn't pulled an all-nighter on the street in ages. In my younger years, before I was a dad, it was easier to do. Not easy, just easier. But age and adaptability have slowed me, so the long tilts are rare. And looking back, even at my best, I am not sure they were ever a great idea.

But one commotion riffed into another, one significant conversation bumped into the next, and one crisis moment was swallowed by a bigger one. Sure enough, the sun rose and I was still there. Feeling my age and then some.

My feet were numb. My brain was too. I could go no further. Heading north on Yonge Street towards my pickup truck, I finally surrendered my last puff of steam, several blocks shy of my destination. I flattened my shoulders against a mirrored storefront and slid to the sidewalk. Just to rest my eyes for a few moments before carrying on.

I woke some time later to the broom shoves of a disgruntled shop owner. Just like so many of my friends do every day.

I rubbed my eyes, stretched long, and rubbed again. With the world slowly coming into focus I caught sight of a peculiar image: a fluorescent orange sleeping bag directly across from me, on the other side of four lanes of slow-moving traffic, curled up in an abandoned alcove.

Chapter 23

It is incredible what ends up on the street, donated to a mission by well-meaning people. Rainbow-striped toe socks, "I'm with stupid" t-shirts, baby blue tuxedo pants with navy piping. The list is endless. Mindless gifts of charity that side closer to cruelty than kindness when surrendered at a mission drop-off. To make matters of dignity worse, it always seems like the most ridiculous junk ends up with those who are mentally ill.

Not only was this sleeping bag electric orange, but from my vantage point it was stiff and shiny, just like "pleather." I had never seen this bag before. I wondered if I had ever seen the body beneath it. None of the belongings surrounding it were recognizable, so I guessed it was someone new. New to me, that is.

I had already done the fool thing and stayed out far too long—something I have warned my team and various outreach workers across the country never to do. Hard to say why I did. Pride? Guilt? Necessity? Stupidity? Sorrow? Most likely a composite of them all. Why didn't matter anymore. My emotions were raw. Catching myself off guard, as I stared bleary-eyed across the street, I began to cry.

How could there be another one? Where are they coming from, and why does it never ever end? Can there be no end to it?

Rhetorical questions that drip with self-pity. Blubbering questions I knew better than to ask. But nearly two decades of fulltime street involvement hit the wall that morning, and what oozed out was not pretty. But God had plans for my ugly moments, as he has on countless occasions. Just as a loving parent might discipline a child with a time out, God sat me down at the foot of the world's longest street and made me wait.

The stores had opened, the stock market bell had rung, and the streets began to bustle with executives, shoppers and tourists. But I did not move. I just watched the orange bag and imagined the life it cocooned, pondering its likeness to those I had known so well.

Names, faces, voices and gestures poured down around me. Bittersweet gifts that had been unwrapped in the sneaky passing of time. Seasons and scenarios that God had cautiously given to me, back-dropped by graffiti and behind trash bins.

Samuel? Could there be another Samuel in that crazy sleeping bag? Starting out on the street believing it would be just one night? Two at the most. When Samuel entered street life he had already skipped three grades of school. He was a genius. When he finally left the street he could barely form a sentence. As I had seen so many times before, the cheapest and most available addictive escape in street culture murdered his brain cells daily as he spent hours on his knees behind parked cars, getting high on gas fumes.

Or maybe inside was someone like one of the "summer six." I once lost six teenagers to suicide in six weeks. Young people I had poured myself into, believing I could help. But one after the other they died, each one taking a piece of me with them. Guilt, sorrow, anger and confusion overwhelmed me. My heart broke that summer in ways that I have never fully healed from.

A big bedroll indeed. Could two be inside? Huddled tight for warmth and protection? Vita and Raymond were reborn in my memory. Both completely deaf. Shocked, elated and frightened in succession, all within the first sixty seconds of meeting me. I had learned sign language many years before while serving at a camp for deaf children. I knew what they were saying: "Yay!...maybe he'll help us?" And then, "Oh no...maybe he'll hurt us." On the streets, hearing is much more than simply one of the five senses—it is the ultimate watchdog. Vita and Raymond never left one another's side. One would stay awake while the other slept, and vice versa. Two-as-one like I had never witnessed before. Sad and beautiful. And silent.

Perhaps it was another Jack? Gentle Jack who convinced me to take him back to his far-away home, because the street was eating him up and "maybe dad has changed." Reluctantly, I did. That same night his father beat him with a hammer. Should guilt be a sin, then I am this world's greatest sinner. I have never forgiven myself for taking him back. Everything in my gut told me not to. Now it's too late to ask for his forgiveness.

Or the Colonel? "Please Lord," I prayed, "not one like the dignified Colonel." He used to sit at the edge of the lawn in front of Queen's Park. He would hobble up University Avenue on his canes, wearing his spit-shined war medals with pride, and then he would rest facing the flag. At his feet was a cardboard box and a sign that read "God knows I did what I could." Queen's Park is the site of the Ontario Legislature, named in honour of Queen Victoria by the Prince of Wales in 1860. The Colonel, looking old enough that he could have been there when Edward VII named it, was proud of the Maple Leaf and loyal to the Union Jack. Fought for his homeland, yet had no home.

Ellen! Yes! Most of all, I could imagine Ellen. Wild and enigmatic Ellen. Now she was one who would actually seek out a sleeping bag like this and wrap herself in it as a badge of honour. An absolute "here-I-am, deal-with-it" personality. One who might insist that every homeless person should be in one, so the world would take notice. Charismatic and opinionated when anyone was watching, and simply a little girl when they were not.

Suddenly, the mummy began to squirm. Someone or something was coming up for air. I stood to get the best angle.

No Ellen of any kind. Not a stately Colonel, a two-as-one, or a "summer six." Nothing of the sort. Poking her head out, with the widest toothless grin I have ever seen, was a tiny old woman who looked just like an apple-faced doll. Her thin grey hair stood in every direction. Her head darted back and forth like a bird on a wire. And she began mumbling to the world with giggles and twitches the moment she emerged. She looked just like a cartoon character. Absolutely adorable.

I stood against the store window and watched her for a long while. Whatever was going on in her head was far more interesting, amusing and life-giving than what was passing her by.

Her little round head bobbing just above the pumpkin bag made me feel many convoluted things. While I was happy for her liberating other-worldli-ness, I was intrigued by her abandon, fearful for her safety, and sorrowful that her life story was likely lost forever.

Lost stories are among the greatest of all tragedies on the streets. This wonderful woman had lived no less than three-quarters of a century. Had she known love? Lost love? Raised children? Had grandchildren? Taught school? Maybe Sunday School? Suffered war? Saved lives? Who knows. But, after run-ning her paces over life hurdles and mind hurdles, she ended up here. Alone and relegated to a discombobulated chat with herself.

Sadly, people with severe mental illness are greatly over-represented in the homeless population. It is estimated that approximately one-third of those who are homeless in any large city in North America suffer from severe mental dis-orders, and that number almost doubles among women, middle-aged and older. The issues are complex, with many suffering from concurrent disorders, such as addiction or post-traumatic stress disorder on top of mental illness. Many have no contact with family and friends, experience massive barriers around employment and shelter opportunities, are often in the poorest health of all who are homeless, and tend to remain homeless for longer periods of time. Worst of all, they are the most stigmatized and alienated of all people, on the streets or off.

After several minutes of chatter to the wind, she stopped and sat back in the deep orange folds. Her bottom lip took up half of her denture-less face. She jerked her head back and forth like a chicken to watch the people passing her by. She was tucked back just far enough from the sidewalk that those in a hurry would only notice her by the time they were almost past her. Those who did see her would often do a dramatic double take. Those in pairs tended to snicker and elbow one another, while picking up the pace. Some acted the way people do at a haunted house wax museum: a yelp of fear, then grand laughter. And of course, a great many just pretended they didn't see her at all. Not pranksters and smart alecks. Just everyday people. People representing all kinds of faiths and compassionate belief systems. The same ones who cry at sad movies and recommend meaningful books.

Soon a mom came, carrying more trendy shopping bags than she could manage with her little girl, no older than six, tagging behind, sucking a red lollipop. As the frustrated mom tried to reach back for the little girl's hand while juggling her purchases, string handles and ribboned sacks slid through her fingers. Flustered by the inconvenience, she stopped in a huff and set them down at the curb to reorganize right in front of the giddy old street woman. The shopping mom bent to her designer bags and boxes facing the street, with no clue of the one behind her. I felt like I was hanging on for a Candid Camera segment.

This goes in the big bag, these go in the small bag, "stay right here" and "listen to mommy," she fussed forever, as though solving issues of world peace. All the while, her little girl stood behind her and watched the old woman in the plastic orange sleeping bag.

After several minutes of unsuccessful problem solving, another woman approached the flustered mother. A friend! A hug. A "long time, no see." And some extra hands to solve the parcel puzzle.

While all this was going on, the little girl and the old lady had begun waving to each other. Then the child would do something like shake her head, and the old woman would imitate her. Little girl's hands on her head, old woman's hands on *her* head. Little girl's hands over her eyes, old woman's hands over *her* eyes. A game. A sweet little game of monkey-see monkey-do. Six years was too little to jade the little blonde in pigtails. She could still see a person with feelings. A person who might like to play. A person who might like a friend. A person worth noticing.

I had been watching for almost an hour, and the only person to stop, the only person to care, the only person to extend a moment of grace or offer dignity was a child being neglected by her mom.

What followed was the stuff that hope is made of. While mom and friend yapped over the purchases and prices, unaware of their surroundings and the child, the wee girl stepped towards the old woman, met her eye to eye, and handed her the sucker. The little old lady held it with her bony thumb and forefinger, right in front of her face to get a good close look. She smiled from ear to ear, and plopped it in her mouth. Once upon a time, even she had been six years old. Some people live an entire life and never get to see a moment so pure. So innocent. So tender. So socially wrong and eternally right.

The fruit of the Spirit described so beautifully in the New Testament by the apostle Paul (Galatians 5:22,23) offers a contrast against simple "acts" of charity. Even understood as such, do we really know what to do with them? We know we like them. We know we want them. But so often we get caught up in the idea that we can simply teach them and learn them. *Love, joy, peace, patience, kindness, goodness, faithfulness, gentleness and self control.* But this little girl was not working from memory. She was simply living them out. And my blessing was to bear witness.

The withered old woman took a long, gleeful taste. Then she pulled the candy stick over her gums and offered it back. Just as the little girl reached out to take it—a shriek! Mom had finally turned. Her daughter had wandered four or five steps away and was sharing saliva with an ancient creature, less clean than the family pet. The mother lunged at the girl, whisked her from the ground, and whipped the guilty lollipop onto the street. Her friend saddled up the packages, and they raced away. The moment popped like a bubble.

For over an hour that sweet old survivor had shown no other expression than a larger-than-life smile. But as the child vanished out of sight in the grip of a woman who thought she had saved her baby from a witch, so did the old woman's smile. That exaggerated smile literally flipped upside down, just like in the cartoons. "Sad" the way it is drawn in comic strips. Further doodles would certainly have penciled in a heart breaking in half.

One of the all-too-common misconceptions about mental illness is that those who suffer from it feel pain and joy less, or differently, than those who don't. So untrue. So tragic an assumption. But an assumption not made by a little girl with the ability to see what so many others miss. Contrary to society's typical notion of mental illness and what to do with it—she inherently knew that the juice squeezed from the fruit of the Spirit is meant to be shared with everyone. Every single one.

With the self-absorbed women and cherub out of sight, the old woman crept out from her strange bright cover. She scurried to the curb, reached into the street, plucked the candy from the roadway, scurried back, plopped it back into her mouth—and smiled.

Recapturing the taste of one pure moment.

Epilogue   Bag Ladies, Beggars, Bums and God

When Elvis came on the scene curling his lip and twisting his hips, introducing the world to rock-and-roll by sandwiching it between gospel classics, he rattled a lot of cages inside and outside of the entertainment spotlight. While music has touched hearts, kept stories alive and shaped psyches throughout history, this poor boy did his new thing at the dawn of the technology and communications speedway, warbling directly into living rooms around the world. He created the tipping point in North America when young impressionable minds would collectively agree to watch the world and make decisions under the vast influence of pop music.

With much less grace, but greater abandonment, the likes of Jagger and Richards knocked those same rattled cages off their stands during their prime. Hendrix tried to melt them. Joplin rolled them barefoot through the mud. And an endless stream of fascinating and perplexing frontmen and women have booted those same social, political and religious cages around the world stage for decades, hoping to leave a mark or dent worth noticing. Though Lennon and McCartney actually tried to release something from them (and debatably, they successfully did) while giving them a good hard shake throughout various states of consciousness, without question, only Paul Hewsen (a.k.a. Bono) has ever come close to convincing the mass mainstream that what's inside the rattled cage is more important than the cage itself. Bending the ear of 15-year-olds on french fry duty at McDonald's and the highest-ranking political world leaders at the same time. A very wide net.

This was no more evident than during U2's 2005-2006 Vertigo tour, in support of the album *How To Dismantle An Atomic Bomb*.

On Saturday, September 17th, 2005 at Toronto's Air Canada Centre I participated in the fever-pitched cheering as Bono called upon the crowd to renew their commitment to humanity and to decisively set themselves against oppression and injustice. I joined in as the audience became a choir and sang united about tolerance and sacrifice. And for a tiny portion of time, I actually believed the inspired crowd had captured the frontman's zeal in some meaningful and lasting way.

But I wasn't more than ten seconds out of the stadium's doors before the charismatic high was stolen from me. I felt like a lame man just healed at a revival service breaking both legs while walking away from the altar.

Two shaggy men sat shoulder to shoulder only paces from the exit. Both had small collection bowls and tiny cardboard signs. I could see them flicker in and out of sight through the legs of a buzzing crowd. I stopped momentarily to watch as the crowd passed them by. Some were angry for the inconvenience of having to step around them, some snickered at their plight, and most just ignored them. Just before I turned away, a young man kicked one of the little bowls into the mob and jeered with his friends. I could see the old man scrambling between the marching feet trying to find his coins without getting trampled on.

A little ways further was an old homeless woman with a shoebox on her lap. Inside was a small white kitten. All kinds of people ooo-ed and aaah-ed at the wee cat. Not one seemed to notice the woman.

Not much further were two homeless teens I knew personally. Some laughed at them, while others brushed by with contempt in their hurry to get to nightclubs and patios. The teens weren't panhandling, begging or asking for anything. They were just sitting and people watching.

All the while I overheard only two conversations. One about how incredible the show was. Two about which pub to gather at.

Somehow, in the seconds between the encore and the house lights coming up, people had forgotten what they had heard and abandoned their collective vow of brotherhood and sisterhood. The only other explanation is even more tragic: that the message of humanity only applied to people far, far away.

The hypocrisy wedged between the 15-minute hike from a stadium seat to the street was treacherous. And not all that different from what often occurs for a great many churchgoers between the benediction of a Sunday service and the church parking lot.

Nothing is easier than singing songs of abundant love. Nothing is harder than living them out. And nothing is more tragic than confusing the two.

I was not much better—landing beneath patio lights with my friends, placing my own order with a midnight waitress. As I looked back across the road, I saw two teenaged girls in U2 concert shirts sitting on either side of an old homeless woman, each with a pizza slice. Hearts still young and innocent enough to have been more than just stirred in the moment. Hope that the next generation is bright enough and deep enough to know that faith without works is dead. And that getting drunk after a few good songs is not going to change the world.

An extra pizza slice and ten minutes to speak kindly to a stranger. Can it really come down to that? I honestly believe that it is in such tiny actions that people can be spurred to greater things and made new. The homeless woman may have enjoyed the pizza slice and been touched by the young voices speaking to her. But chances are, those girls talked about the experience every day for a week. In the end, they received much more than they gave.

In my work, I have met and known the crusaders and activists. I know the petition makers and rally attendees. I know the marchers, protestors and practitioners. The people who make banners, throw bricks and chain themselves to empty buildings. The ones who cover their faces and the ones who strip naked. Ones that inspire me and ones that outrage me. I know the ones who organize prayer rallies in the daytime and bring bag lunches to the streets at night. I know the street preachers and the pavement parishioners. The road nurses and the sidewalk psychologists. I know the mission CEOs and the shelter executive directors. The food source managers, the housing officers and the shelter workers. I know the leaders with the loudest voices and field workers with the softest hearts. Some are the unsung heroes of our day. Some are nuts. Some are both.

This book has not been written for any of them. Initially, it was written for me. Journal notes originally scribbled on everything from bubble gum wrappers to the bottom of my running shoe. A collection of words reflecting merely glimpses of a journey that has flooded my soul with equal portions of joy and anguish. Memories of lives that have changed me, disappearances that have broken me, and losses that visit me in nightmares even now.

It was also written for those who might expect it the least. Not for the activists and bleeding hearts. Not for rock stars, media heroes and award winners. Quite simply, for the parents of young children who wait responsibly in schoolyards every afternoon. For the hard-working buttoned-down employee pacing at the bus stop after a grueling day. For the blue-collar worker who puts in a forty-hour week, stays true to the union and lives for the weekend. For the people who have supper at the same time every night, go grocery shopping every Thursday evening, and never miss the eleven o'clock news. One chapter is for the teenage girl whose greatest interest in life is being at the mall with her friends. Another is for the first-year college kid who lost his pants, his money and his good sense during frosh week, before ever getting to one of his classes. And still another is for the grandmother knitting Christmas scarves for her grandchildren, starting in July.

This book was written to encourage the likes of those two teenaged girls who bought the third slice of pizza. It was written to liberate the people who read about great revolutionaries and social visionaries and consider themselves worlds apart, to urge them to think and believe otherwise. For I believe the greatest revolutionaries in my life—the ones who have shaped who I am, inspired me, and challenged me to seek and find what's best—have understood first and foremost the power of intimacy and community. It is here where bent hope unfolds and is made straight and true.

While it is daunting to take the Son of God as the standard, I truly believe he is the best model. Henri Nouwen said it best in his book *The Wounded Healer:* "Jesus was a revolutionary, who did not become an extremist, since he did not offer an ideology, but himself."

Offering self—whenever, however, wherever, whatever. Perhaps in huge ways you have never imagined. But more likely, and just as poignantly, in small ones. This is both the starting place and ending place.

While there are many great campaigns, movements and missions that deserve our serious consideration and dedication, perhaps the greatest revolution of all needs to begin at our kitchen tables. A revolt against complacency and self-indulgence. Not in the campaign headquarters for some kind of ideological rally, but where selves are discussed and processed most. A Kitchen Table Revolution! There, in the sacredness of the everyday, where children explain their report card marks to parents, where the household bills are processed once a month, where newspaper headlines are read aloud, where family squabbles rise and fall, and where vacation plans are made. It is at the kitchen table where what matters most in our lives gets discussed. Breakfast nooks and serving islands. Coffee tables and TV trays. Whatever serves as the kitchen table, it is there where families, couples, friends and individuals set their priorities and sort out their lives. And it is here where anyone can begin their own intimate and heartfelt revolution.

Surely the world would be turned on its ear, if at every kitchen table the standard dialogue changed even a tiny bit. Of course, this would first require a commitment to have everyone return to the table, to gather unhurried to share in the same meal. But then, once there, the possibilities are endless.

"Let's not just talk about that single parent we barely know at the end of

the street. Let's meet that person. What could we do to be an encouragement?"

"After we talk about what we want for Christmas, let's talk about what we
can do without and what we can do for someone else."

"Son, let's talk about a way you can help the new boy in your grade three
class feel like he fits in."

There are endless ways to discuss single parents, Christmas, new kids at
school, and anything else that is part of your everyday world. The only thing
required for a radical Kitchen Table Revolution is making it a priority, and a
reality beyond the discussion. Of the hundreds of thousands of people who are
homeless in North America, there is a stream of women and men who were once
single parents at the end of someone's street who needed someone to
encourage them. An infinite number of people who had the bottom fall out of
their lives during the loneliness of Christmas. And an endless supply of people
who felt, from a very young age, that they didn't belong anywhere.

As you close this book and reflect on the lives you have met here, perhaps you will decide to volunteer your time through an outreach program,
mission or ministry. Sort cans at a food bank. Make a monthly pledge to a
great work in your community. Read through a charity mailing that you
would normally just toss in the garbage. Roll up your sleeves and get a bit
dirty. Who knows? Maybe for some there is a tug to drop what you are doing
and choose a new path in life. Profound service in a developing country, a
relief effort in a challenging part of your own country, a community-
building initiative in a harsh part of your city, or the giant "I really should..."
at the end of your own street. If you feel any of these things, big or small, I
cannot encourage you strongly enough: do it! The world is in over its head
waiting on people who just need a bit more money, a bit more time, the right
invitation or for the stars to align.

But if all that comes of your time with these pages is that you would consider extending grace with the words you choose, the tone of your voice, and the
look on your face, then I am humbled and thrilled. That we all might recognize
that the value of another person's story is priceless, and that the currency for
our compassion and inclusion cannot be someone having to surrender all the
gruesome details.

If you have made it to this point in the book and you would now summarize
it as a few stories about bag ladies, beggars, bums and God, then I have failed
you greatly. Likewise, I have failed myself miserably, I have failed God
immensely, and worst of all, I have failed the lives shared here immeasurably.

Epilogue

From the first word to the last, my hope was to *reveal* the very art of life. To *introduce* a world of unlikely giants with the warmth of music. To *shed light* on wonderfully sculpted images of strange beauty throughout the book. And in closing, to now *present* a painting. The canvas has indeed been the street. Its smudged background has been homelessness. And the colours have been mismatched hues of sorrow, joy, exhaustion and promise. But with all of my heart, I pray that you feel in some way the final portrait is of none other than you.

Perhaps you as the one who wished for more and is lost trying to figure out what went wrong. Maybe the one who is hiding in places where you hope no one will hurt you anymore. Possibly the one who never stops running in order to survive. The one who is tired of trying. The one doing whatever it takes to make it to tomorrow. The one who is heartbroken. The one who feels ugly. Ashamed. Neglected. Misunderstood. Trapped. Terrified.

Perhaps as you recognize that the portrait is of you, it sits angled close to the light. And in it you find yourself beaming with the joy of a new beginning. Inspired by tenderness. A believer in redemption. A stranger no more. If any of these are images of you, you have read about yourself here.

However, if ultimately I were the artist responsible for the music, sculptures and portraits, then all would surely be doomed. For I truly do believe that the eternal artist of all creation has invited every one of us to stop and experience his handiwork. And to look upon none of his creations without hope. It has been my honour to attempt to reveal, introduce, shed light and present the hidden art of lives too glorious to miss.

And where the world has ripped breathtaking portraits from their frames, rolled them in balls, torn and bent them out of shape, my desire is that we would recognize the only hope for astounding and miraculous renewal. For all of us.

Grace.

Grace.

Grace.

By Steve Bell

"Homelessness is not only of bricks, but homelessness comes from that terrible loneliness that the unwanted, the unloved know along their way. Are we there? Do we know them? Do we see them?"

Mother Teresa

When I was in my early teens, Jean Vanier (founder of L'Arche, an international organization creating communities with people who have developmental disabilities) came to our house for supper. He was crossing Canada speaking in prisons, and my father, then chaplain of the federal penitentiary at Stony Mountain, had the privilege of hosting Mr. Vanier while he was visiting our institution.

I was only mildly impressed that Jean Vanier had left a life of prestige, privilege and wealth to found a home for the mentally disabled, but I found Mr. Vanier himself to be a uniquely curious man. Lanky and rumpled in appearance, he moved slowly and touched deliberately. There was an unusual quietude about him that made you consider whether it was really necessary to talk at all. So I was definitely uncomfortable around him, but pleasantly so, if that's possible. I liked him immediately and immensely, and found myself fascinated by his every gesture.

After dinner, my sisters and I went out into the yard to play, to let the adults talk. I recall feeling sorry I had not stayed inside with the adults when suddenly

I felt a slight but definite change in the air. I spun about on my heels to find Mr. Vanier, sitting quietly on the steps, staring right at me with a look of serene pleasure, a look that suggested he had perhaps never seen anything quite so wonderful. Instinctively, I turned to look behind me to see what it was that so delighted him. But apparently it was me who was causing him joy. We looked wordlessly at each other for perhaps 20 seconds or so before I returned to whatever it was I was doing. Those 20 seconds are some of the most memorable moments of my life. The experience of being seen—really *seen*—and delighted in, is sadly rare, but powerful for a lifetime. My whole being seemed to swell and flourish under his gaze. Truly, I've never been the same. I've known since, deep in my bones, that whatever else may make up who I am, some recognizable portion of "me" is truly good. And I carry that knowledge everywhere I go and into every situation I am given to face. I'm one of the lucky ones.

A few decades later I had a similar experience sitting across the table from Tim Huff at a coffee shop somewhere east of Toronto. We had met briefly a couple of times before, but this meeting was to discuss my participation in a nation-wide conference for street workers that Tim was chairing. We discussed the particulars of my contribution, we discussed music, we discussed family, ministry and all sorts of other mutual interests, but all the while something seemed vaguely familiar. It was the way he looked at me as we talked. He looked pleased, as if he was seeing something wonderful, and I kept wanting to turn around to see what he was seeing. But again, apparently it was me. Tim was visibly experiencing something quite separate from the value of the words exchanged and the utility of our relationship. Tim was *seeing me*, and recognizing me as one of God's beloved. And because he knew, so did I. Lucky again.

So it didn't surprise me at all when I first read the manuscript for this book, to immediately discern that this would be a book about seeing. Seeing past the external decoys folks tend to set out to protect their broken and tender hearts. Seeing past the tragedies and triumphs that give shape to a person's unique story. Seeing past the lies that turn that story into a destructive force. And seeing, finally, the preciousness that can only be described in one word: Thomas, Amy, Smoothy, Correen, Richard, Desmond...Jesus?

It's a wonderful thing to be truly seen; powerful for a lifetime. And it must be equally wonderful to be able to see. I have a suspicion that the capacity to see need not be rare, or assigned only to a handful of selected ones. I suspect it is simply part of what redeemed humanity looks like.

Two humble lines of scripture from John's gospel have often whispered to me to pay attention. Some of John the Baptist's disciples ask Jesus, "Teacher, where do you abide?" More literally, *where do you have your being?* Jesus simply replies, "Come and *see.*" Later, Nathaniel is astonished when Jesus seems to know something of his character. "How do you know me?" Nathaniel asks. Jesus answers, "I *saw* you while under the fig tree."

These pages you have read have been a gift—precious moments when you have been able to truly *see* the individuals whose stories are depicted through the eyes of Tim Huff. But how much better still that we would learn to see on our own?

The word *benediction* means "blessing." One definition for benediction is the following: "the advantage conferred by blessing; a mercy or benefit." As you close the pages of this book, my prayer is that you would be conferred with the mercy, the benefit of the following blessing:

May you be seen—and know it.

In turn, may you see—that others too might know.

So be it.

Steve Bell

Steve Bell is a two-time Juno and multi-award winning singer-songwriter whose life has revolved around music from his earliest years. He is also the co-founder of Signpost Music. His celebrated career has yielded many highly-successful solo albums, concert videos and an extensive touring schedule throughout North America and the world. Steve has a deep concern for issues of poverty and homelessness, which is reflected in both his songwriting and his personal involvement in, and endorsement of, several poverty reduction and awareness campaigns and community-building initiatives.

One of the thoughtful suggestions that arose from an early Bent Hope focus group discussion was that I think through a meaningful way to help people process what they might be feeling as they read through the chapters of Bent Hope. In response, I invited 23 talented and interesting people to think through and write prayers of reflection—artists, writers, leaders and visionaries. 23 people that I greatly admire and appreciate. While they are greatly accomplished in their fields of work, art and ministry, they have been invited to write these prayers primarily because of their authenticity and ability to communicate. As much as anything, they represent parents, grandparents, friends, siblings, co-workers, neighbours, and most of all—people doing their best day-to-day.

Just as the original Bent Hope manuscript was being completed, I was invited to be an "artist" in Signpost's on-line Village. Signpost's mission is to encourage Christian faith and thoughtful living through artful word and song. I love that.

It is a great honour to be able to share these special prayers with you. I know that some readers will engage the prayers enthusiastically, while others may check in on them simply out of curiosity. Either way, my hope is that there might be something in one, several or all the prayers that resonates with the hearts and souls of those who go to them.

For chapter-by-chapter prayers of reflection for the book Bent Hope, please go to: **www.signpostvillage.com/timhuff** and simply click on the Bent Hope tab.

All the very best, Tim.

Since 1944, YOUTH UNLIMITED (Toronto YFC) has been reaching out to, caring for, and investing in the lives of young people in the Greater Toronto Area from every culture and walk of life. Placing the highest value on grace, trust, hope and truth, YOUTH UNLIMITED specializes in guiding young people to "one more chance" when it appears there are no more—while recognizing and valuing them as God's own children. YOUTH UNLIMITED is committed to helping young people attain their full-life potential. In the context of caring relationships, YOUTH UNLIMITED seeks to foster whole-person development—intellectual, social, emotional, physical and spiritual.

Tim Huff began fulltime work with YOUTH UNLIMITED in August 1987, pioneering Frontlines Youth Centre in the turbulent north-west end of the city.

By 1991, Tim had begun seeking out homeless youth in the downtown core who were too afraid, uncertain or untrusting of adults to seek help—those so deeply wounded that they would likely remain "hidden" before seeking the assistance of a shelter, drop-in centre or any kind of meal program.

After a decade of intensive street work in the darkest corners of the inner city, in 2002, Tim gathered a small team and developed YOUTH UNLIMITED's Light Patrol. With a commitment to caring for both the immediate and long term needs of homeless youth, Light Patrol trains, equips and sends out teams of street-workers (staff and volunteers) to be among homeless youth wherever they are—on the streets, in alleyways, under bridges and off-ramps, in parks—focusing on rebuilding trust and guiding young people towards healthy adult-hoods. While Light Patrol's focus is on homeless and street-involved teenagers, they also come alongside many adults and seniors surviving the streets.

Youth Unlimited and Light Patrol

In the course of the Light Patrol's outreach among Toronto's street youth, the team encountered many young people involved in the sex trade. Through these interactions, it became clear that there were few services available to help this most vulnerable group leave the hidden and debilitating underworld that is the sex trade. In response to this need, in 2005, Light Patrol launched the Safe Light program; a specialized outreach among teenagers involved in, or vulnerable to, sexually exploitive or life-changing circumstances—activity or risk of involvement in the sex trade, victims of sexual abuse, facing sexually transmitted diseases, and those facing teenage pregnancy or parenting.

Portions of the author's proceeds from this book will go to YOUTH UNLIMITED in Toronto, and its Light Patrol outreach. Light Patrol is just one of YOUTH UNLIMITED's diverse outreaches and programs. Links to information about YOUTH UNLIMITED, and the Light Patrol program can be found at:

www.signpostvillage.com/timhuff

CASTLE QUAY BOOKS